"There is only one handicap —
the loss of the inner power of the mind.
Why, you don't need hands; you don't need legs;
you need courage, that's all." — Michael Dowling

Library of Congress Catalog Card Number 80-68001
ISBN 0-935476-06-7

Printed in the United States of America by
North Central Publishing Company
St. Paul, Minnesota

Tributes to Courage

edited by

Kathryn Christenson
and
Kelvin W. Miller

published by

Courage Center
3915 Golden Valley Road
Golden Valley, Minnesota 55422

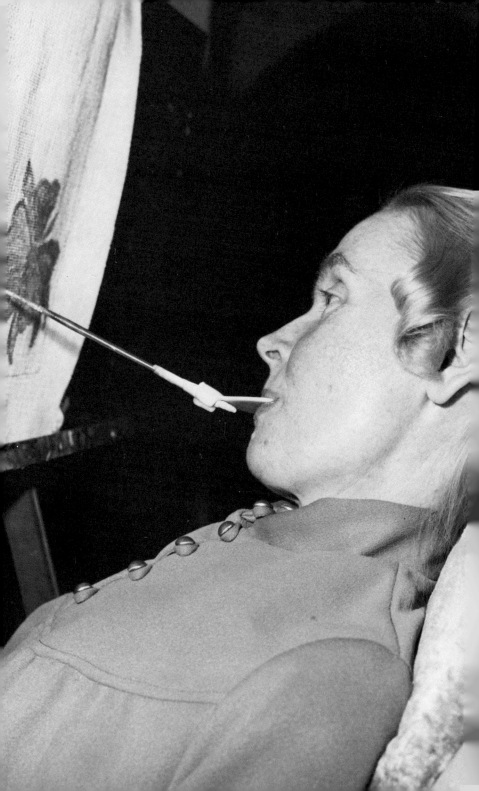

DEDICATION
Margaret E. Anderson
1927–77

Tributes to Courage is dedicated to the memory of Margaret E. Anderson, Minneapolis artist whose courageous spirit and creativity have been an inspiration to all who knew her. Paralyzed as a result of bulbar polio in 1953, she mastered the art of painting by holding the brush in her mouth. She generously shared her artistic talent and her enthusiasm for people.

Margaret was a consultant to the committee that planned Courage Residence for adults with disabilities, and she served as first director of the Residence. At the time of her death in March, 1977, she was involved in setting up enrichment programs at Courage Center for people with disabilities.

As founder and president of the Kenny Institute's Women's Auxiliary, Margaret organized the first annual International Art Show by Disabled Artists. In 1973 she received a Rose and Jay Phillips Award for individuals with physical disabilities who have made outstanding contributions to the community.

Margaret wrote, "After the body stops growing, it is time to develop the spirit. So I will store up treasures that will keep — for I shall not pass this way again." Margaret's words and her memory are still alive, offering encouragement, strength and hope.

Opposite: Margaret Anderson

TABLE OF CONTENTS

ACKNOWLEDGMENTS

We gratefully acknowledge the cooperation and assistance of several people who have helped bring *Tributes to Courage* to fruition.

L. M. Brings, Minneapolis, long-time supporter of Courage Center, was the initiator whose imagination and enthusiasm spurred the book's production. His many friends contributed generously to its publication.

Kathleen Davis, Wilko Schoenbohm and Mavis Voigt, members of the Courage Center staff, were indispensable to the project. They cheerfully provided the advice, consultation and support which facilitated the entire effort. Photographers Candice Jackson and Liza Fourré provided many of the fine photographs in the publication.

Contributing writers graciously consented to lend their time and talents in bringing the stories of courage to life on the pages of the book.

Family members and friends of the thirteen individuals featured in the book kindly offered comments and suggestions with documentation and factual detail.

We thank everyone who has aided us in any way. It has been our pleasure to be associated with Courage Center and its loyal friends.

Kathryn Christenson
Kelvin W. Miller
Golden Valley, Minnesota
June 1, 1980

FOREWORD

by
Itzhak Perlman

This book deals with the stories of thirteen severely disabled people. In each case, the reasons for the success of these individuals are the same: determination to succeed, proper environment, proper parental support and proper attitudes on the part of others.

The handicapped person faces a number of barriers in addition to the handicap itself, such as architectural barriers which stand in the way of day-to-day living and attitudinal barriers which keep the public from believing that handicapped people can mainstream into society. Attitudinal barriers are most profound and are extremely difficult to break through.

People are quick to label a handicapped person "courageous" if that person is an achiever. While courage plays a role in each life, this book is really about attitudes: the attitudes of parents, friends, employers and schools toward people with disabilities. These attitudes make or break a handicapped person's ability to achieve.

The stories demonstrate that given the proper chance, persons with disabilities can achieve their full potential and become contributors to society, rather than being dependent upon it.

Opposite: Itzhak Perlman

MICHAEL DOWLING

by

James Martin

Even as a boy, Michael Dowling fought, and people marveled to watch him. His father, a carpenter, was very strong and loved to box. He taught young Michael how to use his fists. In 1877 when Michael was eleven years old, he worked as a cook's helper on a Mississippi riverboat. On landings between St. Louis and St. Paul, raw crewmen would bet Michael could whip any boy his size. When he won them money, the whooping, roaring boatmen picked him up and hugged him. He won eleven bouts for them that year. For himself he won a rugged education.

Michael John Dowling was born in Huntington, Massachusetts, on February 17, 1866, to parents he would later describe as "poor, but Irish." His mother, who wanted him to become a priest, died when he was only ten years old. Dowling's father drifted West from town to town, exposing his son to frontier America. In St. Louis the boy gathered coal along railroad tracks. On the riverboat he helped the cooks, and fought. In the streets of

Opposite: Michael Dowling   13

Chicago he sold flowers and newspapers. In Minnesota he lugged water on a wheat farm, until the winter of 1880 brought events that changed his life.

At the age of fourteen, Dowling left his father. Intent upon becoming a rancher, he herded between five and six hundred head of cattle, at $1.50 a head, for settlers near Canby, Minnesota. The fourteen-year-old boy, with his pony, had sole charge of the herd.

On the day before he was to deliver the cattle, the air filled with ice particles as fine as sifted flour. The snow froze about the muzzles of the beasts in suffocating masks of ice. Tan and strong from living like an Indian on the open prairie, Dowling moved among the frightened beasts all day, breaking the ice-masks from their faces with the butt of his whip. He kept at his job all night and all the next day until the storm subsided. Most farmers who cared for their own stock in that storm lost cattle. But Dowling brought his entire herd through the storm without losing a head.

Possessing the pony, some small savings, and nine head of cattle, Michael dreamed of becoming a great cattleman. But first he decided he needed more schooling, which was arranged at nearby Canby. Before winter set in, he yearned to see his pony one last time, an animal he loved as only a boy without a family could.

So, one December afternoon in 1880, Michael hitchhiked a ride from Canby, on the back of a lumber wagon driven by two farmers, to see his pony at a farm nine miles away. The farmers sat in front, Michael in back on an empty soapbox.

Minnesota was sparsely settled in those days, its dirt roads wandering across open, fenceless prairies. Without weather predictions, the farmers and their young companion had no idea they were traveling toward a swiftly approaching snowstorm. Open prairie blizzards were dangerous, especially at nightfall. Even walking from their houses toward their barns, farmers had been known to become lost, wandering about in the snow until frozen to death.

Without warning, a gray wall arose from the prairie before them. Too late to turn back, the farmers drove on and in minutes they were swallowed in snow so thick they could scarcely see the horses' heads. Losing their direction in the swirling whiteness, the farmers panicked and whipped the team into top speed. Dowling described the events that followed, some years later.

"As we careened along we came suddenly to plowed ground, and when the front wheels struck the first open break, the jolt sent me and my soap box clean over the side of the wagon. The men on the seat didn't know I was gone and I was too stunned by the fall to cry out. Even if I had, they couldn't have heard me above the noise the wagon made rattling over the frozen furrows.

"I must have come to myself almost immediately, because I yelled at the top of my voice, but the men didn't hear me, of course. There I was, alone in the storm. I ran after them as fast as I could go, but the noise of the wagon died out completely. I tried to follow the track in the snow. But it filled up so fast I had to feel for it with my hands; it wasn't long before I lost it altogether.

"I wasn't really frightened, only rather cross because of the inconvenience I was being put to. I was young and strong, and I knew the country thoroughly. I thought that by keeping my shoulder to the northwest I would surely come to a railroad; then I would follow the track back to Canby.

"To my surprise, I found no railroad. I went on and on, getting pretty tired, and my face and hands and feet were beginning to ache with cold. I hoped to stumble onto one of the few farmhouses of that section. After a while, sure enough, I came to a woodpile. I knew there must be a house nearby.

"I also knew, however, that a dozen paces away from the woodpile it would be easy to get lost again. After thinking it over, I climbed to the top of the pile and, taking sticks of wood, I threw them one at a time as far as I possibly could, turning a little at each throw, so as to cover every direction from me as a center. Each time I listened for the sound of an impact on the wall of a house. No sound came.

"Then I climbed down again, and taking an armful of the wood, I walked about fifty feet against the wind. There I repeated the process of throwing wood in different directions. I did this over and over, each time reserving one piece to throw back to the woodpile, so the sound would guide me to it again.

"Finally, I missed hitting the pile! You would think I could have followed my own tracks back to it, but the storm had wiped them out in the few minutes spent throwing sticks. Now I couldn't find the woodpile itself!

"I knew that somewhere close by was shelter, warmth and safety, but in which direction? I had to keep struggling on, however, for by that time my hands and feet were numb with cold and I knew that if I stopped, the end had come for me. I did not intend to let it come yet, if I could help it. I stumbled blindly, in one direction, then another, until suddenly I came to a straw pile.

"That offered at least a chance of shelter, and I dug my way into it, head first. I hoped I could last in there until the storm let up. Most of the time I felt very comfortable, but I knew what the nice drowsy sensation meant. Comfort was occasionally broken by a wave of bitter cold which started at my ankles and twisted upward around my body like a corkscrew. I knew that I was freezing, but I was determined not to freeze without a fight. All I could do was lie there and fight off the sleep which tempted me almost irresistibly. It was about as hard a fight as I ever made, but I hung on.

"When I felt sure that night must be over, I wormed my way out of the straw—and there, just above the horizon, was the red blur of the sun. Nothing in the world had ever looked so good. I spotted, not more than a half mile away, a familiar farmhouse.

"Hope rushed back and I scrambled to my feet, but I fell. Several times I tried to stand, but each time I fell. Then I realized I couldn't feel my feet any more than if they had been stone. I could see them, but as far as sensation was concerned, my body ended at the knees.

"I struck my hands together to try to restore circulation. That sounded queer, as if I had struck two blocks of wood together. How surprised I was when I looked and saw they were white and rigid, as if made of marble.

"Plowing through the snow to the house was like walking on stilts. There was no pain, just the trouble of keeping my balance. I passed the woodpile, and as I came to the house, I saw in a spot where snow had blown away, one of the sticks I'd thrown last night — two feet from the house."

A farmer's wife who knew Dowling opened her door and gasped to see what the night of fifty degrees below zero had done to the boy. Half his face was frozen still, one eye open and fixed, and the other half was smiling, with an eye moving naturally. He stumbled in from the cold, too relieved to imagine what lay ahead.

Immediately she filled a tub and a washboiler with ice-cold water to thaw his hands and feet. Pain, far more intense than the freezing, accompanied the thawing. As the frost left his flesh, it formed ice casts around his limbs.

Days later, after examining the clearly marked, discolored flesh, a doctor decided that multiple amputations were the only chance of saving Dowling's life.

Two weeks after the freezing, in the Canby home of James Larson, Dowling was chloroformed unconscious on an oilcloth spread upon the kitchen table. When he awoke five hours later, he had parted with each leg below the knee, the left arm below the elbow, and his fingers and half the thumb of his right hand. One of the three doctors whispered to another, "He can never survive such an operation."

"You liars!" shouted Dowling. "I'll live longer than either of you!"

Heavy snows darkened the Larson windows that winter. Dowling felt like he was sick and in prison. Some friends, like the three girls who came to sing, tried to cheer him. Others tried entertainment, such as the Larson boy who played cards with him. With his cards stuck between the closed pages of the family Bible, Dowling pointed to those he wanted played. Yet without a mother, father, brothers or sisters, his spirit plunged. "There were days," he said later, "when I felt as if the whole foundation of things had dropped out and when I rebelled with my whole soul against the raw deal life had given me. At such times, I cursed my own strength of will that had brought me through the storm and the strength of body that had made me survive the operation."

At a party for him on his fifteenth birthday, again Dowling

17

overheard whispers: "Poor boy, isn't it dreadful! He'll be helpless all his life. He'll have to be dressed and even fed by other folks. Too bad he didn't die!"

These words cut like little knives. Dowling turned away and brooded angrily: "I hate pity. I won't be like that. I won't be an object of charity. I won't be laid on the shelf for the rest of my life. I won't, I won't!"

By spring, medical care had consumed all his savings, forcing him to sell his cattle, and, when that money was gone, his beloved pony. That night, he wept until morning.

His money gone, Dowling was brought before the Yellow Medicine County Commissioners. Since no institution for people with disabilities existed then, the chairman proposed that a farmer take care of him for two dollars a week for the rest of Dowling's life. Ole Daley, an old Norwegian member of this three-man board, said, "Well, don't let's be in a hurry about this. Michael, what do you think?"

"Mr. Daley," he said, scarcely able to contain his humiliation at the chairman's proposal, "If you will give me one year at Carleton College and buy me a pair of artificial legs, it will never cost this county another cent as long as I live!"

"Well," stammered Daley, "You can't back that up, boy. That's just your sayso."

"But I mean it," the boy replied.

At first flabbergasted by the boy's bold counter-proposal, the board voted two to one to send him to Carleton for only two terms. After that he would have to fend for himself.

In September of 1883, this young man who had raised himself on riverboats, wheatfields and prairies, mounted the college steps, his new wooden legs squeaking in their leather harnesses. This was the only chance he would have "to learn how to learn," he said. "I knew that if I could find out how real study was done, I could go on by myself. I picked out tough subjects — algebra and Latin — and buckled down to them with all my might."

After his year at Carleton, Dowling supported himself by teaching in frontier country schools, named Stony Run, Hawk Creek,

18

Clarkfield and the Sioux Agency. In the winter, he got to school by wading through snow on ill-fitting artificial legs. "I knew that if I was going to play a man's game with other men, I would have to take care of my handicap myself and not use it to gain favors."

During summers he worked at anything to earn a living — painting the Canby Courthouse fence, selling book subscriptions door-to-door, running a roller skating rink, even learning to skate himself. He was never ashamed of earning his money, except once. Selling maps door-to-door, he also sold photographs of himself showing his disability. A friend purchased one and tore it up in front of Dowling. Dowling never traded on his disability again.

The Minnesota frontier offered a variety of career opportunities, and Dowling was an opportunist. After three years of teaching, he became principal of East Granite Falls High School, and in 1888, he became superintendent of Renville County schools for the next three years. Growing interested in politics and newspapers, he and a friend founded a newspaper, *The Renville Star*. He sold his share of *The Star* in 1890 and resigned as superintendent to travel throughout the North and West selling life insurance.

In two years he was back in Renville. He repurchased *The Star*, also buying *The Farmer*, merging them into *The Renville Star-Farmer*. He ran a series of stories accusing a Minneapolis financial firm of fraud, precipitating an investigation that resulted in the firm's eight million dollar bankruptcy. From the story's wide publicity, Dowling launched another career — this one in politics.

In 1895, he married Johanna (Jennie) L. Bordewich, daughter of the ex-postmaster of Granite Falls. Their first child, a son, Michael John, died in infancy. Michael and Jennie eventually had three daughters, about whom he once quipped, "I am happy to say that when a man has his legs frozen off . . . he does not pass on to the next generation the same condition. The girls all take after their mother — they are good-looking."

But back to politics. Dowling often said that he had a lot of brass and was sorry that he did not have more. He displayed what brass he had one day at the national Republican convention in Philadelphia, which he was covering for his newspaper. Chancing to overhear two politicians discussing who would make a good national secretary, he interrupted to say, "Gentlemen, I know just the man you are looking for — his name is Michael J. Dowling." For the next two years, Dowling served as the Republican National Secretary.

He was never ashamed of his disability. On the contrary, he used it for fun and advantage at every chance. In 1900, he was sent to the Philippines as a member of a United States government commission on education. For whatever the reason, the religious and governmental potentate of the archipelago, the Sultan of Sulu, was bored to pieces by the prospect of listening to this commissioner. To gain the Sultan's attention, Dowling removed his left arm and cast it at the Sultan's feet. The ruler was startled from his lethargy. Then Dowling removed his legs and clattered them to the floor before the astounded sovereign. With his remaining arm, Dowling reached for his head, threatening to unscrew it. The captivated Sultan would now listen, provided the commissioner would reveal the secret of his dismemberment.

Dowling returned to Minnesota to engage in state politics, real estate and banking. Elected to the State Legislature in 1901, he was nearly a unanimous choice for Speaker of the House in his first year. Popular among politicians, Dowling earned a reputation for honesty and hard work, a reputation supported by friendly newspaper editors throughout the State.

In 1920, Dowling, with help and encouragement from Elks Club members and Rotarians, sponsored legislation providing $250 each for eligible children with physical disabilities to attend a special school. This school for youngsters with disabilities was first located in an old church at 1805 Dupont Avenue North, on Minneapolis public school property and was furnished with Junior Red Cross funds. In recognition of Dowling's sponsorship, the Minneapolis School Board broke with precedent and named this school after a living person: the Michael Dowling School for

20

Crippled Children was born. It was subsequently moved, in 1924, to the location on West River Road in Minneapolis, where a beautiful new facility was built, honoring Michael Dowling.

The First World War saw thousands of disabled soldiers returning to the United States, which, like other nations of that time, was woefully lacking in knowledge of rehabilitation. By now, Dowling was a remarkable, self-made man. He had risen above his disability to become a teacher, a superintendent, a United States Commissioner, and a Speaker of the Minnesota House. He currently was president of the Olivia State Bank. Yet once again, a new desire stirred within him. At fifty-three years of age, Michael Dowling began his last career.

It started the day he visited maimed soldiers at Fort Snelling, Minnesota. The men, mostly amputees, were called into the first ward. They straggled in listlessly, expecting another in a dreary series of addresses.

"Boys," said Dowling crisply, his eyes sparkling, "I came expecting to meet a bunch of cripples. But so far as I can see, I'm about the only first class cripple in the room! How many of you have lost both feet?" None had. "How many have lost both arms?" Again, none had. One man had lost an arm and a leg. "Well, you boys aren't in my class at all. I've lost both legs, one arm and most of the other hand."

The men were startled, some suspicious. He challenged the skeptical to rap on his wooden limbs. No one came forward. Instead, they grew quiet and receptive. This was a new experience for Dowling. For the first time, he sensed he was among people who were vitally interested in him as a person with a disability. He began talking about his disability more openly than ever before. He talked to them about battles he had won, battles he had lost, and how he had won his war. He transformed them all for the moment, and some, perhaps, permanently. When he stopped, enthusiastic soldiers crowded about him, bursting with questions. Dowling left Fort Snelling, knowing that he had touched them and that they, quite unexpectedly, had touched him.

Word of his speech spread, and he was asked to talk again and again. He spoke to those damaged by the bloodiest war history had ever known. He spoke to men with a leg off, an arm off, both hands off, both legs off, an arm and a leg off, and some stone blind. He spoke throughout the United States, England, Scotland, Wales, France and Belgium.

It was a night in New York, however, in the Hippodrome, before an audience of more than five thousand people, including a thousand wounded soldiers, sailors and marines assembled by the New York chapter of the Red Cross, that Dowling delivered the speech he had been preparing throughout a lifetime.

"You boys lost a leg or an arm fighting in a great cause; I lost mine just fighting a blamed old blizzard, and there's not much glory in that," he shouted out to men sitting in wheelchairs, boxes and orchestra seats. "You are the handicapped, handicapped because you had the courage to win the war, handicapped by the Hun who couldn't win it." His solitary voice rang out, "Why, the luckiest day in my life was the day the surgeons carved me up. Right there I made up my mind to do something — not because of any ability I had — I simply said, 'I will,' and I did. You boys will do the same, I know."

The bitter blizzard of thirty-nine years before had taken his limbs and replaced them with something greater, something that he now tried to pass on to these newly-disabled men. Hushed, they leaned toward him. Once again, Dowling opened his heart.

"Handicap? What's a handicap?" he cried. "It's just a chance for a good, honest fight! When I was a boy, I fought with boys. When I became a man, I simply changed my foes. Men, if you have a handicap, act as if you hadn't. Try to forget it. Above all, don't let others keep it in their minds.

"Handicap? There is only one handicap — the loss of the inner power of the mind. Why, you don't need hands, you don't need legs, you need courage, that's all. Our bodies, what do they count? A good deal, of course. Yet a man may be worth a hundred thousand a year from his neck up and not a dollar a week from his neck down."

22

Wiping perspiration from his face, he softened his voice. "Affliction turns some into sponges. Sponges merely soak up pity. Sponges never get anywhere. We talk about the winds of adversity, well, the hardiest trees are those that have been buffeted about. They don't grow in hothouses or sheltered nooks."

His voice rose again. "There are plenty of things worse than losing a part of your body. You may lose — you do lose, sooner or later — a part of your heart, somebody or something to which your heart clings. And you have to fight that fight, too. If you are a real man, or a true woman, you won't lie down and give up without a struggle." He paused, then declared, "My friends laugh when I say I feel sorry for a cripple. I am not bluffing — I thank God I am not a cripple."

He walked to his chair through an ovation. Secretary of State Charles Evans Hughes, the meeting's chairman, who later became Chief Justice of the United States, rose to declare, "That was the best American speech I have ever heard!"

After his European speaking tour ended in 1921, an exhausted Dowling came home to Olivia to rest. His heart failed, however, and he died in a St. Paul hospital on April 25, 1921.

On the day of his burial in Olivia, simple signs that covered locked doors on storefronts said, "We mourn our loss." Mourners came from all parts of the Northwest to the small town — by special train from the state capital in St. Paul, by automobile, by wagon, and by foot. An estimated 300 people stood bareheaded on the windswept lawn of Dowling's home to hear a service so simple as to be scarcely a ceremony. From Dowling's flower-filled front porch three clergymen, each of a different faith, spoke brief prayers.

Not a word was uttered in Dowling's praise. All those present, from the smallest child of the Dowling School, to the highest state official, already knew him. And because they knew Michael Dowling, the man who had been knocked down but never knocked out, they silently vowed to fight their own battles harder than they had ever fought before.

23

KARL ANDERSON

by

Jane Rachner

As a young man, Dr. Karl Anderson earned at least thirty-two medals by breaking records on the high hurdles, but the biggest hurdle he ever had to take, one which could never be photographed, even in slow motion, was a hurdle for which no medals are given.

No bronze medallions, silver cups, or plaques would be adequate recognition for what it means to cope for fifty-five years with a speech condition and a paralyzed right arm and leg. To be struggling to relearn every word you ever knew and to be dragging useless appendages with you wherever you go, when once you gloried in their strength, would surely constitute a difficult cross to bear.

But Dr. Anderson has borne it well. The hurdle of adjustment that he mastered has also been a hurdle for his wife, Crystal, requiring that she possess similar patience and endurance. For both of them the challenge began the afternoon of November 9, 1925.

At that time Crystal Anderson was twenty-four years old. As a new bride she was expecting to face only the pleasant hurdles of homemaking and child-raising. For slightly over a month she had been sharing the joys of honeymoon and marriage with her handsome husband, a surgeon one year older than she.

The man with whom she had fallen in love was strong in intellect, character, and physique. Always athletic, the young doctor had, during his college years, been the captain of the University of Minnesota track team. As champion of the high hurdle he had been the first athlete in the State of Minnesota to win a place on an Olympic team.

He had attracted notice as an outstanding University of Minnesota student not only for physical but also for intellectual accomplishments. Because of his scholarship and his reputation for levelheadedness, he had been chosen for membership in the order of the Grey Friar, a senior honorary society.

As Karl himself puts it, "The Karl Anderson of autumn, 1925, thought he had the world by the tail. He had won national and international acclaim as an athlete and was headed for success in his chosen career. He was already doing major surgery at Abbott and Eitel Hospitals in Minneapolis."

On the morning of November 9, after the young couple had been in their apartment but a week, Karl went off to work, feeling well and fit, and performed two scheduled operations before noon.

Picture him an hour or so later back in his office, seated at his desk, with pen poised ready to write a prescription for a patient. Then picture his wife meanwhile tidying their apartment, perhaps polishing a wedding gift coffee pot. Would either of them have believed that in the next moment their world would come crashing down around them?

Suddenly Karl's pen slid from his hand as a stroke paralyzed his entire right side, took away his power of speech, and rendered him unconscious. During an eleven-day period of unconsciousness following his stroke, Karl's doctors at Eitel Hospital told the Minneapolis *Journal* that he was dying, so this is of course what the paper reported. Fortunately, the paper was wrong. Dr. Anderson has miraculously outlived three University of Minnesota Department of Neurology chairmen who have cared for him.

Sometimes it appears, from looking back upon an individual's life, that a system of signs or symbols is instrumental in the person's career. If such a pattern emerges in Karl Anderson's life, the significant symbols seem to be aquatic.

The first symbolic incident took place in 1924. It happened in Paris, France, where Karl, having been granted six weeks' leave of absence from his internship at Abbott Hospital, was competing in the Olympic games as a member of the United States track team. He had reached the finals in the high hurdles. The race was on, and he was five yards in the lead. Suddenly an isolated puddle loomed just ahead of him on the track, and Karl's foot hit it, causing him to do the splits and setting him back in the race by several yards. In spite of the fall Karl picked himself up and continued the race, even managing to come in fifth.

How symbolic that puddle was! It showed that a sudden misfortune can eliminate a big advantage. And it also showed that perseverance in the face of a potential catastrophe can keep an accident from resulting in total defeat. This incident foreshadowed a more serious event that life would soon have in store for Karl.

But for the time being, Karl Anderson was part of a lively scene. Karl was feted in England when the Duke of York, later King George VI, awarded him the Wimbledon medal in high hurdles. When Karl and other hurdlers lunched with Douglas Fairbanks, the event was publicized in the newspaper. The producers of a film featuring the famous American movie star wanted the public to know that only an Olympic star would be good enough to train their leading man, Douglas Fairbanks, to hurdle a hedge. Who in London, or anywhere else for that matter, would have predicted that a year later the star athlete would be hospitalized and close to death?

Close he was for the eleven days following November 9, 1925, but then Karl surprised everyone by regaining consciousness. Later he refused to stay in Eitel Hospital for as long as his doctors wished him to. He insisted on getting out for Christmas and then persuaded his doctors to let him stay in his apartment and later go to Florida with his wife and brothers. Karl's father and six brothers comprised the Anderson and Sons Company, cement contractors, and they had been asked to supply cement to a tourist development called Miami Shores. Thinking Florida sun would be good for the invalid, the Andersons took Karl and Crystal along and rented a small cottage for them. There Crystal spent all her time helping Karl learn to walk and talk again.

At first Karl could see no progress. Terrible discouragement and the feeling of being a millstone to his wife and his relatives made Karl despair. Lying awake at 2:00 a.m. one morning, Karl came to a decision that he could no longer burden the people he loved. A canal a block away from where he and Crystal were staying became fixed in his mind as an avenue of escape.

In Karl's words, "I stealthily moved from bed to floor. Although I could hardly walk, I managed to get out of the cottage. Then I half crawled, half stumbled all the way to the canal. Reaching the edge I suddenly stopped and turned, feeling a hand on my good arm. Crystal was there. In a soft voice she said, 'Karl, you're not a quitter.' My desperate reply was, 'I was only thinking of you,' but the moment was a turning point, and I never again considered suicide as a way out." The canal, momentarily a symbol of escape, became a symbol that love and courage can conquer frustration and suffering.

Another aquatic symbol was the ocean, metaphor for vast untapped potential. Crystal would sit on the beach with Karl every day working tirelessly to help him learn to walk and talk. The oceanside with its vista of unlimited aquatic expanse became the setting for the first small, slow successes that made Karl realize that recovery might really be possible and that the future might hold some promise.

Though hope began to spring in Karl's heart that he might recover some of his power of speech, he could not have envisioned that thirty-nine years later he would be addressing a conference of the Northwestern National Life Insurance Company in Carmel, California. Having attained by then a position as vice president and medical director of the company, Dr. Anderson was asked to speak at the opening meeting of the Half Million Dollar Club, the elite of the company's sales organization. The title he chose was "The Potential for Greatness," and even though the speech was primarily about the company's growth, Karl, mindful of a parallel growth of his own that he could not have accomplished without his wife's help, alluded to Crystal in the opening part of his speech:

"If it were not for his good wife, this would-be surgeon might still be confined to a wheelchair, but with her gentle insistence he fought back, gradually regaining his speech and overcoming the paralysis."

Of course no one, not even Cyrstal, could eliminate for Karl Anderson all the discomfort associated with his stroke. The doctor had accepted the fact that he could never fully return to what he had been. He knew that a career in surgery was out of the question. For a long time he also accepted his doctors' unanimous opinion that he and Crystal would be unwise to have children.

But in 1928 a fourth aquatic symbol became a part of Karl's life, and it symbolized the continuity of life that he would achieve. That was the year that Karl and Crystal bought a cottage next door to her parents' house on Lake Minnetonka. At that time they had no thought that they might have children who would grow up there and grandchildren who might live there or enjoy visiting the lake. What they believed was that each year might be their last together. However, as the years went by, the fear of Karl's imminent death lessened, and the couple began to believe they might be together long enough to raise a family. More than seven years after their wedding they had their first addition to a family which now includes two daughters and seven grandchildren.

Staying alive and creating new lives were significant accomplishments for a man predisposed toward cerebral hemorrhage. But Karl had an even more difficult goal in mind. He wanted to use his life to benefit other people just as he had originally planned to do when he aspired to a career as a surgeon. How could he get back into productive life and play some role in his field?

As soon as he possibly could, a year and a half after his stroke in fact, Karl began to make daily trips to the University of Minnesota Medical School. He audited classes and observed free clinics, but it was not until he mastered the task of making his left hand substitute for his right that he was able to take notes while he listened and watched. Naturally, he was no longer studying surgery. He had turned his attention to internal medicine, particularly cardiology and diseases of the kidney, and he was beginning to hope he might win a University of Minnesota fellowship.

His first request for a fellowship to study for a Ph.D. in internal medicine brought a gruff answer: "Go home, and come back when you're well." Did this crushing response discourage the man who heard it and who knew he would never really be fully well? You would think it might have thoroughly squelched his hopes, but it did not.

Instead Karl redoubled his efforts. Since part of the job of any University fellow in medicine involves lecturing to beginning classes, Dr. Anderson knew he must recover his speech well enough to give lectures. Somehow he managed to do this very thing. He learned to get to the podium, plant his useless insensitive right hand on the lectern, and then concentrate all his pent-up energy on projecting his voice, gesturing with his left arm, and relating with eye contact and contagious enthusiasm to the audience of medical students.

Eventually he obtained the fellowship he sought. He cleverly handled the inevitable verbal lapses which are effects of his stroke that will never entirely disappear. He did it by turning his first lectures into oral completion tests, pointing first at one student, then another, eliciting the missing word as if his lecture had been deliberately designed as such a test. Bit by bit Karl made a place for himself and attained the position of clinical associate professor. For forty-three years he kept this professorial position. The University of Minnesota students learned much from his lectures on heart and kidney disease and gave him their respect, support and affection.

Opposite: Hurdler Karl Anderson

Karl Anderson's service to his profession led to honor after honor. His awards include the Harold S. Diehl award for outstanding service to the University of Minnesota Medical School and to the medical profession. It was presented to him by the University's alumni association. This and many more awards came to Dr. Anderson because he dedicated his life to the welfare of others more thoroughly than many so-called able-bodied men.

He has been a community leader in the field of rehabilitation, working on rehabilitation committees through the years for United Way and for Courage Center. He helped lay the groundwork for the mergers which resulted in Courage Center, and he served on its Board of Directors. The fact that Minnesota has a better rehabilitation climate and better barrier-free conditions than most states is due to the efforts and concern of people like Karl Anderson.

Throughout his life he has had great faith and the help of many people. He is grateful to God for these years of service and fulfillment. He is still active in community groups, church affairs, the Minnesota Medical Foundation, and is a member of the Associates of Bethel College in St. Paul. He is constantly helping other people and organizations get over their hurdles.

People often ask Dr. Anderson if they may write his biography. The story of his conquest of tragic adversity is an inspiring one, but Dr. Anderson resists its being told for anyone's personal profit. It is his intention that any proceeds from the recounting of his life story go to one of the nonprofit organizations with which he has worked, such as Courage Center.

Dr. Anderson has never been content merely to rest on his past laurels, however. In fact he has always been future-oriented. For example, he was ahead of his time in promoting the mainstreaming of disabled persons and also was a pioneer in the field of geriatrics.

He has long advocated the creation of incentives and the elimination of obstacles to the disabled person's efforts to see meaningful employment. While an officer in Northwest National Life Insurance Company, he was instrumental in promoting and supporting the company's decision to continue disability payments to many of the firm's claimants for an entire year after they went back to work.

Long before the government decided to extend the number of years a person can work without facing mandatory retirement, Karl Anderson was advocating and predicting such a change. In a 1954 speech at the forty-second annual meeting of the medical section of the American Life Convention, Dr. Anderson called attention to the problems of the elderly which are so much in the news today.

At that time he said in his characteristically colorful manner, "We may not have reached the point where Marlene Dietrich is the typical American grandmother, but neither is Whistler's Mother, and any attempt, deliberate or otherwise, to relegate the bulk of our oldsters to rocking chairs will be the more tragic because of the untold problems of ill health and social maladjustment which will result."

Dr. Karl Anderson is, and always has been, a man of courage. Life dealt him a blow that would have left many people passively resigned to their rocking chairs. Not Karl Anderson. Living out the early promise he had shown as a young Olympic star, he has not retreated, but continues to move forward gracefully and confidently, taking the highest hurdles.

MERLE BADER

by

Dorothy Collins

For Merle Bader, his body covered by open sores which "hurt like a toothache always," and without hands, the independence of being able to work and make his own living is truly freedom.

It is what keeps him going, he says, and makes his life worthwhile.

Merle describes himself as a "workaholic," toiling long hours, six or seven days a week, at his job at Kost Brothers Ready-Mix. Speak to Merle about courage and he simply brushes it aside and says he owes what he has been able to do to his parents, to his doctors, to others who have helped him along the way.

Never does he say, "Why me?" Quietly he says, "My parents taught me never to feel sorry for myself."

Quiet is the word for Merle, although he is easy to talk to and converses readily. Folks have treated him well, he says, and he can recall only one or two unpleasant incidents. You get the feeling he hasn't let those incidents diminish him.

Merle was born on a farm near Breckenridge, a small city in

Wilkin County in northwestern Minnesota, December 7, 1933, with a disease most people have never heard of — Epidermolysia Bullosa Dystrophica. The disease means that his skin is so paper-thin that it cannot withstand the slightest irritation. As a result, he has sores over all his body and some become infected.

There is no known cure for the disease, and no one appears to be doing any research to discover a cause or cure. Merle thinks the only hope is that a researcher may inadvertently stumble on some of the answers while working on another more common disease.

Merle's brother, eleven years older, has the same condition. Is it hereditary? No one knows that, either, although there may be some link, since there was an uncle who also was so afflicted. But Merle and his brother, Isidore, have two sisters who are free of the disease.

Merle remembers that while he was growing up, his mother each night wrapped his entire body with bandages, as well as that of his brother. The bandages had to be washed over and over again, and she did this uncomplainingly too.

"My mother was a strong person," Merle says. "I never heard her complain of my brother and myself. My parents never let us feel unwanted or a burden. My father never complained about the bills either. I had very unusual parents."

His father met the bills without any outside help until his mother became ill with cancer and his brother lost a hand. "The people at the Courthouse said, 'Why don't you let us help you?'" Merle related. The family finally was forced to accept aid.

In 1955, the family moved into Breckenridge. His mother died the following year. Merle drew disability five or six years. That ended years ago, Merle is quick to point out, and he is entirely self-supporting now.

Merle's hands were lost to cancer that was caused by the disease which afflicts him. His brother has lost one hand.

Merle's education ended with sixth grade at St. Mary's School in Breckenridge, and he remained at home twelve years. There was the security of family life and enjoyment in fishing and hunting. "I was young enough that I didn't have to think about doing something for myself," Merle says.

Then at age eighteen, he awoke to the realization that, "I had to start thinking that my dad was not going to be able to take care of me all my life, and I had better think of doing something for myself. My dad had spent everything on medical bills."

Merle subsequently took tests administered by the State Employment Office in Wahpeton, North Dakota, across the river from Breckenridge, to determine what field he might be fitted for. The results indicated bookkeeping or social work. He also took a series of tests at the Vocational Rehabilitation Center in nearby Fergus Falls, Minnesota. The center considered paying his way through State School of Science at Wahpeton for a year.

He enrolled at the Science School, attended one year and part of the second. It had been a long time since he had been in school and then it was elementary only. "The first quarter, I would have liked to quit, but after that, I learned how to study," he says.

Merle's first job was with a construction company. Four years later when Kost Brothers bought that company, Merle stayed. He remembers the date well — March 16, 1964. He has been there ever since. "I have had a good relationship with the company," he says.

Every evening after work, Merle goes to St. Francis Hospital in Breckenridge to get his body wrapped with rolls and rolls of gauze — a two-hour job.

He works hard and long. "I feel I have to give 110 percent or I'm not satisfied." He takes Tuesday afternoons off to go to Fargo, North Dakota, for a therapy session. And then he usually works Saturdays to make up for it. On Sundays, he may end up going back to work two or three hours. "It's a habit I can't break," he says. "I've got to justify so much work for the inconvenience I cause them."

A typical day goes like this: to the Post Office to get the mail; to the office to open it; write up all the paid on account slips; make up the bank deposit; work on collections; check over invoices and accounts payable; check invoices for errors; work on getting es-

37

timates for commercial jobs; work on getting bid bonds and performance jobs; make sure they are lined up and ready to go; and in-between, "do a lot of running around for parts."

Merle, who lives with his father and brother, spends so many hours working and at the hospital that he has little time for leisure activities.

The exception is the pleasure he takes in his two vehicles, a 1976 Chrysler Custom — "my Sunday car" — and an El Camino pickup. "The most enjoyment I get out of life is driving my car and knowing it's paid for," he says. "I just like to drive around and listen to music." He has a steering wheel knob to fit his hook into, and, with power steering and brakes, he has no problems. He averages 35,000 miles a year.

He travels to St. Paul quite often to the University of Minnesota Hospitals, where his some fifteen surgeries were done. He has always used his vacation time for hospitalization. "I know I'll end up being in the hospital every one or two years," he says. From 1960 to 1975, he had to have a skin cancer removed from his hands nearly every year.

Merle doesn't get downhearted very often. "I can't see any time that I got depressed from my sores hurting," he says. "Probably I get depressed because I couldn't reach the goals I set for myself."

Until recent years, Merle worked not only for Kost's, but also did bookkeeping for other companies on a part-time basis. He remembers starting out part-time at $150 a month. "I think the government has gotten back in taxes what they paid for putting me through school," he says with satisfaction.

Had he gone through high school, Merle says his first goal would have been to be a lawyer and the second, a certified public accountant. Still, he's satisfied with the work he's doing.

He has his own electric typewriter and types with a pencil holder that fits into his hook. There is no secretary at his office, and he does all the typing needed there. He writes with either his right or left hand.

While he was having so much surgery, "The only thing that

kept me going" was the inspiration provided by Dr. W. Albert Sullivan, head of plastic surgery at the University of Minnesota, and Dr. Robert W. Goltz, head of dermatology. "Just being around Sullivan, there was no way I could give up," he says. "Every time I had major surgery, he came into my room the day before, and as busy as he was, he always had time to stop and talk to me."

He goes to University Hospitals for checkups every three months. Now the checkup is in urology, for a kidney stone that is getting larger. He may have to have it removed. If that should occur, the doctors won't know until the surgery is under way, "whether the inside is as delicate as the outside. If so, that would be quite a jolt to the doctors," he said.

He adds that if that should be the case, "I'll either make it or I won't. I don't worry about that. I've lived longer than I expected to." He has considerable faith in medicine. "You can go through a lot and they can still pull you out of it," he comments.

But what keeps him going is the fact that he is useful to society, Merle says. "If I weren't, I don't know . . . if I would have had the will to live. If there is something to come back for, you come back, but if not, I'm not so sure."

Merle's courage in the face of far more misfortune than most people have encountered has been recognized outside his community. In 1966, he was presented with the Rose and Jay Phillips Award by Courage Center for being one of five outstanding Minnesotans whose continuous employment in the face of great handicap represented unusual effort and accomplishment.

The same year, he received the WCCO Good Neighbor Award. He is a member of the Fraternal Order of Eagles.

Merle's philosophy in the face of his unusual handicaps and his contribution to society surely are inspiring to everyone he encounters.

JAMES CARLISLE

by

John E. Tilton

Most, perhaps all, of the several hundred high schools in Minnesota each year select a valedictorian, the topmost scholar in the graduating class. Valedictorians generally are not unique.

But one of the valedictorians of the class of 1957 at Rosemount High School was something special. He was James Robert Carlisle, a cerebral palsy victim who had lived through infancy, childhood and adolescence in a state of complete dependency.

Complete dependency is actually a technical term for a person unable to care for his most elemental personal needs. Carlisle cannot dress himself, bathe himself, or feed himself. He cannot comb his hair. Handwriting is beyond him. His speech is so impaired that only a half dozen people can understand what he says. He cannot walk. Add up all the fingers and toes of both his hands and both his feet and he has only one digit — the index finger of his left hand — which functions.

Yet today Jim Carlisle operates a thriving accounting and tax business with a growing list of more than 230 clients scattered throughout Minnesota.

His friends say, and the record seems to confirm, that he has a mind razor-sharp, an all-consuming sense of humor, an easy, outgoing personality, infinite patience and a determination to tackle and surmount the most monstrous odds. By almost any standard, Jim Carlisle is a successful business man and a good citizen who asks no quarter from anyone and who has made his way against handicaps that, to most of us, seem almost hopeless.

How did this all come about? How was this miracle achieved? What went into the development of this incredibly different, unbelievably effective personality? To answer these questions is to discover the essence of the Jim Carlisle story.

It features a heroine, Jim Carlisle's mother; a hero, Carlisle himself; a pretty, blond ingenue named Carol Linkert, Carlisle's secretary and right hand for the last four years.

It all began November 9, 1936, in a hospital in Tyler, Minnesota, when Lester and Leona Carlisle from the nearby town of Russell, became parents of a baby boy. The boy, as you may have guessed, was James Robert Carlisle.

From the beginning there was worry about the baby. He cried a lot, seemed fretful and did not develop properly. Finally, when he was seven months old, he was taken to a specialist who told his parents the stark and bitter truth. The child's brain had been damaged at birth. He was a victim of cerebral palsy. He would never be able to walk or talk properly.

After the first shock of that discovery, Leona Carlisle and her husband figuratively took a deep breath, gritted their teeth and agreed they saw something worth saving in that tiny little creature. For five years they fought against the mounting evidence of deep physical trouble and then, on an off chance, took the baby to another specialist for an intelligence test. The results were encouraging. Within that crippled little frame was a keen mind with a wealth of potential.

By this time the family had moved to Duluth, to St. Paul and then to Rosemount in pursuit of employment opportunities for Mr. Carlisle, an automobile mechanic struggling to support his family in those years of deep depression.

In Rosemount Mrs. Carlisle, a former teacher with many years of training, went to school officials. She needed help, a special tutor equipped to develop the mind of her crippled son. The response was not encouraging. There were no funds for such instruction, school directors said, and no assurance the board legally could fund such instruction.

Grimly, Mrs. Carlisle went to work. The county nursing service helped. Jim had athetoid cerebral palsy, one of several kinds of the disease, with some vicious symptoms but which, most frequently, developed handicapped folk with an outgoing personality, a willingness to learn and a dogged persistence. One of the child's problems was that he could not talk. Mouth, tongue and throat muscles were semi-paralyzed. Mrs. Carlisle and her nursing service friends developed a long list of exercises to restore life and function to those deadened muscles. There was some improvement, but it came slowly.

In 1947, a new experience opened for Jim Carlisle. He was sent to a private school for crippled children at Jamestown, North Dakota, in the hope that there he might share in the normal classroom give and take denied him in his home tutoring routine.

But that did not work either, for a most unusual reason. Young Carlisle, sheltered in his own home for years, had never been exposed to normal childhood diseases. Exposure came in a vast wave at Jamestown and, with it, weeks and months of sickness. In a single winter, Jim Carlisle had the whole gamut — measles, mumps, chicken pox. So disastrous was the experience that his parents, in desperation, brought him home.

But not before Jim Carlisle had gained a great deal. After a fourth grade year in Jamestown, though ill most of the time, the youngster learned he could compete, that he could fight for his rights and often win. That, he agrees today, was worth all the fretful worry of Jamestown.

That same year, 1947, stands like a beacon in Jim Carlisle's life. It was then that the Carlisles learned that the Minnesota Legislature had approved the financing of private tutoring in the homes of physically handicapped students. Back to her school board went Mrs. Carlisle, asking help for her boy but agreeing the problem was difficult, if, for no other reason, because she alone was able to understand the boy's painful efforts at speech.

"All right," said the board. "We must provide him a tutor. You are a qualified teacher. You, alone, can understand him. Why don't you take the tutoring job?" And that, of course, was the way it worked out, all the way through the youngster's eighth grade.

By that time, a new personality entered Jim Carlisle's life. He was Eugene Olson, today director of audio-visual education in Rosemount High School, who had become interested in the Carlisle case. Olson agreed to assume the tutoring responsibility, plunging into the task. Studying the problem coldly, Olson decided the boy needed work, vast quantities of work in all the disciplines to offset his lack of extra-curricular activity which other children enjoyed.

So he piled the assignments on, watching with growing confidence as the youngster buckled down to his successive tasks and emerged, almost without fail, with a straight A average. One hour each day, Olson would study the results of Carlisle's previous day's work, make new assignments, and then leave the boy to another ten or twelve hours of study.

Was Carlisle, in his senior year, named co-valedictorian because of a misplaced sympathy for his condition? Absolutely not, everyone involved agrees. The boy won the honor fairly by the sheer excellence of his performance.

Meanwhile, he has picked up some other kinds of honors. He has learned to handle a specially-built typewriter, geared for that precious left index finger, though the going is slow, up to several hours for an average letter. He has become interested in three other fields: writing, photography and a fascinating kind of pencil sketching.

Upon graduating from high school, he won a Quill and Scroll journalism award and a special scholarship award from Stockyards National Bank of South St. Paul. In 1977 a Rose and Jay Phillips award for self-sufficiency and independence despite severe physical limitations was presented to Carlisle by Courage Center. This, remember, from an individual whose extremities jerk uncontrollably, whose speech is understandable by only a half dozen close friends, and whose reading is obviously slow because the printed word he is holding quivers constantly with those muscular spasms and it is hard to keep his eyes on track.

Four or five albums of beautiful photography testify to his photographic skill, with a specially designed camera gripped between his legs. Another four or five albums are packed with distinctive pencilled sketches, drawn while twisting sideways in his wheelchair. In the seventh grade, young Carlisle sketched every one of the country's Presidents. There's also a beautiful likeness of Clark Gable and another of Harry Belafonte, scores of still life works and, still cherished by Leona Carlisle, the first recognizably good work he ever produced — of an Indian princess.

How successful, really, is the Carlisle accounting and tax business? Quite successful indeed, despite the fact that it is managed in an unusual way.

After leaving high school, Carlisle took a crash correspondence course in accounting with the International Accountants Society in Chicago, the equivalent of a four-year university course. He never advertised his services, he explains, the business just started growing slowly and kept on until this year it serves more than 230 clients throughout the whole Twin Cities metropolitan area.

Today the business functions through a miniature office in the Carlisle home where the accountant and Ms. Linkert preside with just enough space for a collapsible desk where client conferences are staged. It reminds visitors a little of an airliner cockpit. Two desks are surrounded by instruments and equipment. There is that typewriter, the keyboard covered with a perforated shield permitting Carlisle to rest his whole hand on the machine while that exploring left index finger finds and punches the right key.

There is an old-fashioned adding machine and a new calculator, similarly equipped. There is a one-way telephone with a loudspeaker receiver and no transmitter. (When a call comes,

Carlisle listens and voices his answer to his secretary, who interprets his reply for the caller.) There is a reading machine, tuned to a radio station which records and broadcasts the day's news. Here Carlisle keeps abreast of the day's events, since handling a newspaper is an almost impossible task.

There are other minor items, of course. All are specially designed and equipped for operation by a man battling a continuing series of convulsive movements in all parts of his body.

Tax and accounting clients are asked to fill out a form, providing most information needed to handle their accounting problem. If there are added questions, Ms. Linkert asks them. If the client needs to go into added detail, he is asked to come in for a conference with the secretary serving as interpreter.

It all works smoothly and effectively. So much so that clients keep returning again and again. Included, say Carlisle, are some very interesting people from as far away as Bloomington, Golden Valley and Minneapolis. Some, Ms. Linkert explains, are obviously fascinated by her boss and seem to enjoy their conferences there.

In busy season, a second secretary is added, a part-time worker who helps with routine typing, assists in handling the load of correspondence and generally functions as Ms. Linkert's aide. In those busy periods of the year the two women work different hourly schedules so that Carlisle, for eleven hours or so a day, has at his side a secretary who can provide needed telephone service and other assistance.

What have been the major problems in Jim Carlisle's adjustment? First, Jim will admit, has been the problem of communication. Those persons born with easy speech, find it almost impossible to understand how difficult this area can be, and in ways one might never expect.

Spelling has always been difficult for Carlisle. That is because he cannot pronounce words clearly and, without a clear syllabic pronunciation, spelling was an agonizing trial. "I used the dictionary so much," he chuckles, "that I bought a new dictionary every year . . . for many, many years." It is easier now.

Perhaps the next most difficult problem has been the simple business of transportation, getting from place to place. Within his home, his wheelchair functions well, of course. When he moves elsewhere, he is transferred to a motorized chair, pushed up two aluminum ramps into his van and locked into place for the drive to his destination.

There was a social problem. For most of his childhood, Jim Carlisle lived in lonely isolation because other children, having had little experience with handicapped people, saw him as a strange and almost frightening individual. "No one ever, ever spoke to me," he explained.

That changed a little when Carlisle went to the Jamestown School for handicapped youngsters. There he was no longer the exception, no longer abnormal, but was one of a group of children, each with his or her problem and each with understanding. There, Carlisle learned what it means to be an equal.

Eugene Olson, his high school tutor, added something here as well. Olson brushed aside Jim's protests, insisted Jim could compete with the best, and demanded top performance. Under Olson, Carlisle learned the satisfaction of hard work and the joy of successful achievement.

The problem of complete dependency, of course, has been most overwhelming of all. "Everything was a problem," Carlisle adds thoughtfully, "but somehow, somewhere we've always been able to find solutions."

Through his lifetime, the entire family agrees, the Courage Center organization and its Camp Courage have been a priceless support. Camping with understanding counselors and scores of others with comparable handicaps, Jim Carlisle found real friendship, new confidence and an understanding of his place in society.

At Camp Courage, he learned to swim, with help at first but ultimately by himself. He learned the intricacies of wheelchair square dancing as one of a group wheeling enthusiastically through a set of figures. He went horseback riding, with the aid of a helpful counselor. And, with a group of Camp Courage friends, he took an extended trip through the eastern United States in his trusty van. Three beautiful photo albums tell those stories through pictures taken with Jim Carlisle's own camera.

Jack Isaak of Rosemount, a friend, and Bob Heuer of Brooklyn Park, a former Camp Courage counselor, are both long-time admirers of Carlisle. Each, in a different way, is strongly positive about the whole Carlisle story but particularly about Carlisle's mother, who has devoted her life, both before and after the death of her husband, to her son.

Both Isaak and Heuer emphasize that a deep and abiding faith in the rightness of things is one of Carlisle's most interesting attributes. Sixteen years ago, Carlisle began a series of Christmas letters to friends and clients, narratives of his activities in the year just closing. What comes through, in those beautifully written letters, is the faith and assurance that dominates the man.

In all this, there is a parallel between the life stories of Jim Carlisle and Helen Keller. Keller, an Alabama girl born a century ago, suffered an illness as a baby of nineteen months that left her blind, speechless and deaf. But Keller, except for her blindness and hearing defect, was physically normal and later learned to speak. Carlisle's five senses function normally. His problem is muscular control of his body. Both Keller and Carlisle enjoyed alert and sensitive minds. Both became useful citizens and exciting personalities because of the dedication of lifelong companions.

Those who work with handicapped people argue that every human being is worth saving, no matter what his or her limitations. When the mind is sound, dedicated counselors always can find ways to bring out its maximum potential. That, in essence, is what happened in the lives of Jim Carlisle and Helen Keller. Together, they symbolize what the mission of Courage Center is all about.

ANNE CARLSEN

by

W. B. Schoenbohm

A phrase which appropriately describes Dr. Anne Carlsen's approach to life is "a zest for living." Dr. Anne, as her students, associates, friends, and admirers affectionately call her, is an intrepid human being who, with a great deal of expertise and efficiency, directs an outstanding hospital school for severely handicapped children in Jamestown, North Dakota. She has obtained a Ph.D. degree in Education, conferred upon her by the University of Minnesota in 1949. She has traveled all over the world, is an excellent public speaker, and has done lecturing, writing and consulting for organizations and centers for the handicapped in many countries.

The coveted Rough Riders Award from the State of North Dakota, given to but a handful of distinguished and admired Americans, was awarded to Dr. Anne. She received the Presidential Handicapped American of the Year Award in 1958, and numerous other rehabilitation awards on state and local levels; she drives her own car, to date without accident; she writes beautifully; typewrites; is fiercely independent, and does a

Opposite: Anne Carlsen   51

myriad of other things, all exceedingly well. All of this she has done despite the fact that she is a quadruple congenital amputee with small stubs where arms and legs should have been.

Dr. Anne was born in Grantsburg, Wisconsin, in 1915, a time when it was still customary to isolate handicapped people, rather than try to integrate them into society. She was, however, fortunate to be born into a home where love and acceptance, as well as a profound recognition of her worth as a person, abounded. Her father was determined that she would get the same chance as her four older brothers and one sister to live as fully and productively as possible. It is said that shortly after she was born and family members had expressed concern about her disability, her gardener father took her in his arms and said, "We will wrap her with our love and help her to blossom. I think God has something in mind for her."

Dr. Anne has little recollection of her mother, who died when Anne was only four, but whom she credits with getting her off to the right emotional start in life. However, the dominant force in developing Anne's positive and determined approach to life was without question her father, whose wise homespun philosophy helped to mold Anne's zest for living. He strengthened her self image in early childhood by emphasizing that she was an important human being, that she really had brains and could go a long way. His pride in her every little achievement nurtured her desire to excel. Anne recalls the time when, as a small child, using her little arm stubs, she learned to pick a pin off the floor and how her father lost little time in letting all of his friends and neighbors know what a remarkable girl his daughter Anne was.

Anne attributes a great deal of her zest for living also to her older sister, Clara, who stepped in and became a second mother to her when her own mother died, and to her four older brothers who were always there to encourage, to advise, and to help when she needed them. The love that her parents had exhibited for her was naturally carried on by her brothers and sister and provided the motivation and courage for her to face life cheerfully and assertively.

Anne frequently has remembered her father's admonition, "Anne, having arms and legs missing is not nearly as important as having a good mind. The important thing in life is for you to develop your intellect." She has often quoted her father's saying, as well as the words of another source of inspiration, Minnesotan Michael Dowling, who lived with a similar disability. One of Dowling's slogans was, "It's not what's gone that counts, but what is left."

Anne's father emphasized many times that he never wanted her to let her disability keep her from doing the things that she wanted to do. Like so many immigrants to the United States, Mr. Carlsen was deeply committed to seeing that his children got the best education they possibly could, and this included little Anne. His determination no doubt accounts for the fact that all six of his children were well educated, one of them in addition to Anne getting a Ph.D. degree.

At the same time, Anne's father was very emphatic that he never wanted to see her taking unfair advantage of people because of her disability or exploiting her disability to get special preference. Frequently, later on, Anne would laboriously climb two or three flights of stairs if no elevator was present, rather than have someone carry her. The viewpoints of her father became cardinal principles in Anne's life. She was determined not to let her disability stop her and not to utilize it to gain any unfair advantage.

This spirit of courage and "you can do it" which was a part of the Carlsen family conviction soon pervaded the whole community. Dr. Anne has often said that there are advantages for disabled individuals growing up in a small town because acceptance seems easier there. Acceptance of Anne was transferred from parents to family, to friends, to the community, ultimately to all who learned to know her.

The children in Grantsburg loved Anne because she loved them. They liked her because she was open about her disability and their curiosity toward it. In fact, Anne feels that children are more accepting of differences and handicaps than adults. Children are more inquisitive than they are cruel, particularly if their curiosity is satisfied.

Anne loved sports and entered into the game of baseball with enthusiasm, usually ending up being catcher. She likes to tell the story of an incident that happened later on when her brother Albert's son was four years old. The boy had been given a dart game for Christmas. When Anne suggested that she might like to join in the game of darts, his response was, "But Aunt Anne, how can you play darts?" "Let me try," she said, and she was soon astonishing her nephew by her accuracy in throwing darts with her arm stubs. His surprised comment was, "Aunt Anne, you can do anything without hands." A short time later he brought his friends in to have them see his amazing Aunt who "could do anything," even play darts, in spite of her disability.

At the age of eight Anne was pronounced educable by a school psychologist and was allowed to try public school. She solved the problem of writing by holding a pen between her two arm stubs, and her penmanship continues to impress people today who wish they could write as well. Anne exhibited a great capacity for learning and breezed through grade school two grades at a time. At twelve she was ready for high school. About this time Anne was fitted with artificial arms, but because she had acquired such remarkable dexterity with the use of her arm stubs, she soon discarded them as being too cumbersome and a hindrance rather than an aid to her independence.

It was at this point in Anne's life that her father, who had been a gardener at the Royal Palace in Copenhagen, Denmark, and had opened a small florist shop in Grantsburg, accepted a position as gardener at Gillette State Hospital for Crippled Children in St. Paul. One of his major reasons for the move was the increased educational opportunity he envisioned for Anne. Although he was reluctant to leave a community in which Anne felt secure and knew most of the 900 inhabitants, her father convinced her that it was a real advantage for her. Never one to back away from a challenge, she welcomed the move with great anticipation. Again she was accepted by her peers who, together with her brothers, helped her to and from school in a specially-adapted wagon.

At fifteen Anne underwent surgery for the amputation of her one, short deformed leg so that she could be fitted with artificial legs, which greatly improved her mobility, increased her stature, and gave her a feeling of independence greater than any she had ever known. Unlike earlier surgeries further from home, this one was at Gillette where friends and family could visit her, and her father was able to bring a fresh flower each day.

Upon finishing high school at the former St. Paul-Luther Academy and College in St. Paul, Anne continued there for two years of Junior College, and then transferred to the University of Minnesota. Here she faced some real challenges. She was now one among many! While some of her advisors, like Dean Edmund G. Williamson, strengthened her faith and hope, and encouraged her in her aspirations to become a teacher, others more discouraging suggested that teaching was simply out of the question for Anne. Undaunted, she finished the University of Minnesota in 1936, graduating with honors in a class of over 500.

With the country at the peak of the great depression, Anne was unable to find a teaching job. For two years she tried other jobs but felt frustrated and unfulfilled. However, Anne never gave up on a teaching career, feeling that without it she would never be able to prove what she could do with the education she had so laboriously acquired.

It was in 1938 that Anne's life and that of this writer converged. At that time he was head of a small, struggling school for handicapped children in Fargo, North Dakota, which later developed into the well-known Crippled Children's Hospital School in Jamestown, North Dakota. A professor at Concordia College who knew Anne recommended her for a position at the school, stating that she had a physical disability herself, which should enable her to be a most effective teacher. Anne was called for an interview. It soon became obvious in talking with Anne and discovering her enthusiasm for living and her desire to teach, that her disability, however severe, was really small compared with the positive, dynamic force of her courage, her faith, and her determination to live creatively and to encourage others.

Anne's first job with the little residential school, established in an old unused college building and struggling desperately to stay alive in the midst of the devastating depression of the 1930s, paid her $25 a month plus room and board. Although it was not much of a job according to today's standards, for Anne it was the opportunity she had always dreamed of, and her march to the top of her career had begun. Of that first job she once said, "When I got it I was suddenly flooded with the realization that I had found my niche, and I was home professionally, knowing what I wanted to do and what I wanted to achieve."

Two years later the school was moved to Jamestown, North Dakota, where a new school was built in a beautiful seven-acre park. After serving as Principal and Child Guidance Counselor, Dr. Anne became Administrator in 1950. The preceding year she had received her Ph.D., having obtained a master's degree from Colorado State College in Greeley, three years previously, by going to summer school in addition to her teaching position.

Now firmly established as head of an outstanding residential school for children with severe physical handicaps, Dr. Anne finally felt that she really belonged and that she could maximize her education, her philosophy, and her personal experience by helping other handicapped individuals to take their rightful place in society. Having been strengthened throughout her life by family and friends, and being a resilient spirit herself, she was determined to do all she could to help others achieve a similar outlook on life. Dr. Anne is convinced that a person's attitude toward his or her disability is generally far more influential than the disability itself.

Anne is a member of three honorary societies, Phi Theta Kappa, Delta Phi Lambda, and Psi Chi. She has traveled extensively, one year being sent to Australia by Rotary International to help create an awareness and appreciation of the potential of disabled individuals. She has appeared on numerous television shows, including the Lawrence Welk Show. Welk, a fellow North Dakotan, has been a supporter of the Crippled Children's Hospital School through the years, and is a special friend of Dr. Anne's. She has been the subject of numerous newspaper and magazine articles, and she also has written many articles on rehabilitation.

Opposite: Dr. Anne encouraging a young patient

One of Anne's great attributes has been her natural acceptance of her disability, which she attributes to the fact that she was loved and accepted by her parents. If parents can face their child's handicap, the child will find the handicap easier to face. Anne has never been bitter. She has never felt God selected her to be handicapped or punished her in any way, or that her parents were at all to blame. She does not feel that it was God's will that she should be handicapped, but rather that in this world of imperfections, out of so many children born each year, a number will be handicapped, and a number will be born with congenital amputation. Given this fact of life, Dr. Anne believes that each person must try to make the best of the situation. There is plenty left to enable individuals to lead full and useful lives.

Dr. Anne admits that there are things that she would like to do which she cannot. One of them, she confesses, is sports. Since her childhood she has been interested in physical activities, but realizes that because of her delicate balance and the use of crutches and artificial limbs, there are some activities she cannot undertake. She loves to hike, but must limit the distances she goes because, as she says, if she walks too far, which she sometimes has, she pays for it later.

Anne does not agree with the philosophy that God makes some people handicapped so that other people will recognize their blessings. She says, "Life is a precious gift for which people should be grateful, and they should not wait until they see a handicapped person to be reminded to count their own blessings."

Dr. Anne remembers not only her family with a great deal of gratitude, but many others who have influenced her. One of these was the family doctor, Dr. E. I. Bunker, who delivered her and who believed in her from the start. It is said that after Anne was delivered and Dr. Bunker was pacing the floor describing the delivery to his wife, she remarked, "Maybe it would have been better if that baby had not lived." "Never," Dr. Bunker is supposed to have replied. "She'll make it, and we're going to help her."

Anne remembers that this was not just an idle statement, but that the Bunkers became a second family for her, doing things for her that her family was financially unable to do. Dr. Bunker would take Anne to the county fair, carry her around, show her the interesting sights, take her for rides, and see to it that she had some of the fun other children had despite her disability. He helped her get used to being with people, being accepted by people, and being accepting of herself. "Because of him," she states, "I became more secure, more self reliant, and was helped to a greater faith in my potential as a person." Dr. Bunker's prediction that, "What Anne lacked physically, nature had compensated for by giving her other talent," became a prophetic statement.

Throughout history there are people who, because of strength of will, character, faith, indomitable spirit, and the timely assistance of loyal friends, rise to the top and improve the lives of many others. Dr. Anne is one such person who, despite, or even because of her disabilities, has enriched and encouraged many others, inspiring them to live more fully and abundantly by concentrating not on that which is gone, but on that which is left. She has a true zest for living. It is fitting that The Crippled Children's Hospital-School in Jamestown is being renamed The Anne Carlsen School for the Physically Handicapped. Fellow North Dakotan Lawrence Welk has said, "I admire Dr. Carlsen so very, very much. Here is a lady who had so much against her, who not only succeeded in developing herself beautifully, but is giving so much to others as well."

KAREN CASPER

by

Carol Lacey

Determination . . . stamina: Karen Casper grew up with them and now she is fortifying those qualities in other disabled persons trying to make it on their own.

"Once I say I'm going to do something, I most often follow through, I don't stop short," she reflected during an interview one bitter cold winter evening. She was relaxing by a blazing fire in the White Bear Lake home that her parents, Ted and Rita Casper, moved into just before she was born.

Karen, second to the youngest of seven Casper children, was just under a year when cancer of the lymph glands struck. As cancer cells multiplied, they penetrated the spine and pinched the nerves. Although the cancer was arrested, the nerves never regenerated. Karen's balance, stomach, bowel and bladder suffered some damage, but her legs were the most obviously affected. Although she does have a little movement in her legs, she knows she will never walk.

From the beginning, she never had the idea that she should be catered to or get special treatment just because she was a paraplegic. "I was always well incorporated into the family. They didn't treat me differently or exclude me from family activities," she said.

Thus, even though she knew she would be the only physically disabled person at Lakeaires Elementary School, she started her public school education with the attitude, "Why not?"

Karen needed that. Even though she participated as fully as she could in the school program, she felt keenly what it meant to be left out. "Kids can be extremely mean the way they exclude you. . . . Growing up can be devastating," she said.

Even though this was long before the days of architectural barrier sensitivity, the Lakeaires school staff did their best to make the facility accessible. It was easy at the start because the lower grades were on first floor. And, by third grade, she was tall enough to learn to manage stairs by herself. That took care of things until sixth grade. Surgery that September lengthened Karen's heel cords so that she would not walk on her toes. Bone blocks were inserted in her ankles so that her feet would not flop over. That meant, however, that she was in long leg casts for seven months, nearly the entire school year. She still went to Lakeaires — with the help of two teachers who carried her up and down stairs each day.

After grade school, Karen continued her education in the public system, graduating from Mariner High School in 1974. A month or so after graduation, the Minnesota Department of Vocational Rehabilitation (DVR) came to her with an offer. "We'll pay for your schooling if you figure out a plan."

It didn't take her long to decide on nearby Lakewood Community College. She did not want to give up her part-time job at Sears and, besides, there were not many schools still accepting applications in July.

She found work at Lakewood was rather routine. "I wasn't a good traditional student," she said. Still, she made sure she had the courses she needed to get an Associate of Arts degree.

Karen's two years there were nearing an end, and she was

starting to think about what she might do next, when a Lakewood counselor told her about Metropolitan State University, "a great school for those who didn't like traditional classes."

"At the time, I thought I was taking the easy way out," Karen recalled. "Once there, it was the hardest I had ever worked."

Schools she attended in the past had mapped out what to take. "Do this," they told her, "and you'll get this."

It was different at Metro. If she wanted a degree with special emphasis on counseling and human services, it was up to her to figure out what she needed to do to get it. "If you can prove your plan to us, we'll approve it," she was told.

By the time she graduated in 1978, she had completed not only the necessary competencies, but two internships, one at Gillette Hospital, the other at Courage Center. There she essentially laid the groundwork and established the community contacts for the job she would later occupy.

Karen moved directly from being a student at Metro to Mankato State University, where she began a master's program in vocational rehabilitation counseling, receiving her degree in June, 1980. The Department of Vocational Rehabilitation suggested that this might be a good idea, but had no funds to pay for Karen's training; however, a federal grant given to Mankato State helped to underwrite much of her graduate school costs.

For two or three days a week during an entire school year, Karen drove the long round trip from her home in White Bear Lake to Mankato and back. In addition, she combined her field experience for her master's degree with her work as discharge planning specialist at Courage Center. That part-time position became a full-time job in August, 1979.

Karen works particularly to develop independent living plans: housing, attendant care, budgeting, transportation, financial resources, whatever severely disabled persons need to make it on their own. She has also worked to develop a manual for independent living.

She loves what she's doing. "I can use my creativity," she said. "It allows me flexibility to try anything."

While she does not consider herself as one of the more militant disabled, she does feel a strong sense of responsibility to help break down barriers that exist. She realizes that because disabled persons have been isolated for so long from the community, it has been hard for some of them to know how to respond to being part of the public, at least at first. "The fear of the unknown can be overwhelming at times," she said, "but a positive attitude and a pleasant approach can go a long way."

Yet Karen knows that these things will not be enough. She is encouraged that legislation is forcing the public to pay attention at last to the needs and concerns of disabled persons. The public may have given lip service to these needs in the past, saying "Yes, they can be part of the community."

Now, however, "we're beginning to see action behind those words so that people with severe disabilities can participate independently in the community," she said.

Yet there is a long way to go. She is disturbed, for example, that the system encourages disabled people to stay on assistance. The conditions for medical assistance are the "biggie," she said. Most quadriplegics need this help to pay for the attendant care they require to help with dressing, hygiene and food preparation. On medical assistance, however, the most they can earn is $256 per month. To afford this care on their own they would need to gross, at a minimum, $18,000.

This makes it impossible for quads to get the work experience they need to qualify for the higher-paying jobs that would enable them to be financially self-sufficient, Karen said. "How are they going to get into a job paying $18,000 a year, even with a master's degree, if they have no experience? Yet the law doesn't allow them to gain the experience."

Karen has accomplished a great deal for a woman in her mid-twenties, and she is comfortable with the direction of her life. "I move into situations as I feel confident to take on more," she said.

As she counsels others toward achieving their goals, she is working on some long-range goals of her own — like owning a wheelchair-accessible home someday.

Opposite: Athlete Karen Casper

As involved as she is with her work, Karen is anything but all work and no play. An active and illustrious athletic career began at age seven when her parents enrolled her in the Courage Center Red Cross handicapped swim program at St. Paul's Wilder Pool. At age nine, she started going to Camp Courage. By the time she was fifteen, director Jim Olson had noticed her. He told her of his plans to get a swim team together for competition. "It might mean traveling for those who do well," he said.

That was the incentive she needed. Back for her junior year at Mariner High School, she talked to a teacher, Bill Erickson. "He had worked with teams, but wasn't coaching that year," she said. "He said he'd work with me on weight training."

That entire year she lifted weights. Then she contacted Jim Olson again. He entered her in the May regional meet; she won and went to national competition. In swimming, she placed first in breast stroke, second in freestyle, third in back stroke; in track she scored third in the sixty-yard dash. Selected then as a member of the national team, she went on to pick up four firsts, four seconds and three thirds in competition in England and Peru.

From then on, Karen's athletic record kept getting better and better. In 1975 she scored five firsts and a second nationally, in 1977 eight firsts and a third, in 1979 she made a clean sweep with seven firsts; in the course of these national achievements she set four national records. These performances in swimming and track, of course, qualified her, year after year, for international competition in places like Mexico, Canada and Brazil. After six straight years of chalking up impressive lists of first, second and third place awards in international meets, however, she had to pass up attending the 1979 events; she just could not rationalize being gone two of four weeks during a critical summer course in her graduate program.

Each year she found she had to work harder. "It's getting very specialized," she said. "The quality of competition is good. You can't train for a couple months, then go in and expect to win."

Karen did not mind working. "If you do it, you might as well do a good job, not a halfway effort," she said.

In contrast to the loneliness of swimming, being a member of the Rolling Gophers women's basketball team sponsored by Courage Center is anything but solitary. The same Jim Olson who had sparked her interest in training for swim and track competition asked her in 1975 to be part of the basketball team. "I wasn't really interested in doing it at the time," she confessed. But she figured she'd do it anyway and has stayed with it, practicing at least four hours a week with the team, playing a schedule that has more than doubled from the early seasons of ten games, and helping win a national women's title.

In her education, her work, her sports, Karen Casper's family has been behind her one hundred percent. "All the way along, they have been completely supportive," she said. "Because of the positive attitude in my family setting, that's what I expected from others. For the most part, I got that." With her determination and stamina, Karen will continue to instill a spirit of courage in the people around her.

STEVEN K. CHOUGH

by

Gareth Hiebert

From the window of his office on the fifth floor of St. Paul Ramsey Building No. 3, it was a long way to South Korea for Dr. Steven Chough.

Back there forty-five years was a small boy two-and-a-half years old living in Kimchon, for whom the world suddenly became silent when spinal meningitis left him without any hearing.

Then he was at the foot of the ladder.

He has never stopped climbing.

That middle week in January when we met for the first time — and perhaps the last — Dr. Chough was beginning to pack his books, cleaning out his desk behind the doorway marked: "AD-MINISTRATOR" of the Mental Health Hearing Impaired program at St. Paul Ramsey hospital, a program which he, more than anyone else, began, nourished and saw change the lives of scores of hearing-impaired people.

But for him the next rung in the ladder is always the challenge. And he was climbing to one more called, "Director of the Center for Deaf Treatment Services'' at Northville Regional Psychiatric Hospital in Northville, Michigan.

When it is suggested that he has been a Johnny Appleseed, planting seeds of hope and help and techniques to treat hearing-impaired people to live as if they had 20/20 hearing, he smiles and begins to gesticulate in the language he knows best — the signing of letters, words and phrases.

"I am flattered at the analogy," he says through an interpreter, a young woman who was trained at the nationally-known Interpreter for the Deaf course at St. Paul Technical Vocational Institute.

It has been a pleasant triangle these last four years, he says — the proximity of the TVI training program, his program at St. Paul Ramsey and a growing awareness of hearing-impaired people as human beings, with talents, abilities and facility for doing everything anybody else can do, except hear.

"But that," Dr. Chough will quickly add, "is not true. I hear. They hear with their hands and fingers, eyes, facial expressions. Some also hear by reading lips. I do not wish to get involved in the controversy about which method is best. Use everything you can to hear."

And when luck comes your way, use it.

This is what Dr. Chough did long ago in Korea when, after the frustration of having his education and teaching career in a school for the deaf shattered by war, first with the Japanese, then the North Koreans, he "lucked out one day."

Serving as a civilian employee with the United States Army, he made a friend of an American serviceman who took the time not only to learn Korean, but to learn it in sign language. And young Chough learned English, which he added to the Korean and Japanese he already knew, thus becoming multi-lingual without ever saying a word or hearing one spoken.

One day his new friend gave him a 1952 copy of *Collier's* magazine. In it was an article about Gallaudet College in Washington, D.C., the world's only liberal arts college for deaf students.

Young Steve Chough saw it as one more rung in his ladder of life.

"I've got to go there," he said.

And he did, but climbing that one rung wasn't easy. He had to cut through red tape, persuading Korean officials he deserved to be given an exit visa.

There was this soliloquy: "My father wanted to come to the United States when he was young, but couldn't make it because of money. I wanted to show him that his sons could do what he couldn't," said Steve, who did not learn to communicate with his parents until he was eight years old.

But he spent five years trying to get that coveted visa.

All students had to pass three tests to apply for a visa.

Finally, he passed them all and then the captain at the Defense Ministry in charge of issuing the visas had a "nasty attitude toward deaf people."

He challenged Steve's ability to understand English.

"He wrote in English to see if I could understand, and I promptly corrected his grammar. The captain was so embarrassed that he signed the papers and I got my visa right away."

But it wasn't smooth sailing when he finally boarded a cargo ship for the United States. The young Korean got an attack of appendicitis and was late for classes at Gallaudet.

The next three rungs in Dr. Chough's ladder are marked: bachelor's degree, master's and doctorate.

He reached each one, but not without some lesser steps. Late and bewildered when he got to Gallaudet, he managed to survive the first year, then whipped through with a major in sociology and minors in psychology and philosophy.

"Most people with hearing loss do badly in these communication-type courses and very well in math, computer sciences, chemistry, where they don't have to talk to anybody in a daily regimen," he says. Unfortunately, he got terrible grades in math and chemistry, so, "I didn't have a natural aptitude for those."

From Gallaudet he was on his way up to the University of Denver for his master's. There were no interpreters. He couldn't understand any of the classroom lectures, but he took notes rapid fire.

Finally, with sweaty hands and anxious groping for the next rung, he pulled himself up to the master's degree in social work. He was the first deaf person to obtain an M.S.W. in this nation. This achievement led to New Mexico and Texas, where he worked with deaf children as a counselor and then social worker at a state school for the deaf.

When the dean of students resigned, Chough applied for that position. But he was passed over, "because they said I wouldn't do a good job since I couldn't use the telephone."

This attitude is something he abhors. He finds hypocrisy in the suggestion that people with hearing problems should be educated to use their talents and "mainstream it," but can't be taught properly by deaf people.

"Who knows the problems of hearing impaired individuals better than someone who has the same difficulties, the frustrations?" he said that day in his St. Paul Ramsey hospital office. And he diligently pursues this crusade.

His decision to leave Texas for the New York State Psychiatric Institute was a fortuitous next rung up. Or maybe two.

Here he got his chance to work in a program — the first — to provide mental health counseling for people with hearing loss. Nowhere else in the country was this being done, and for four years, Chough counseled in a variety of areas — emotional, family, marriage problems. He also married his wife, Nancy, whom he had met in his Gallaudet years. Nancy cannot hear either. "It has been a wonderful marriage," he laughs.

Always restless, wanting to do even more, Chough decided that in order to be recognized and trusted and respected in his field, he needed a doctor's degree.

"It was," he says now, equally as much "to show hearing people that deaf people could do as well as hearing people. I wanted also to be a model for deaf people — to inspire them."

He chose Columbia University because of its prestige and prox-

Opposite: Chough with wife Nancy and children

imity to his position. Columbia was a reluctant bridegroom. But Chough persisted. And perseverance paid off.

The year was 1970. For eight years he labored on his Ph.D. Then, on May 17, 1978, he crossed the Columbia University stage and added "Dr." in front of his name. This made him the first deaf person to receive a doctoral degree from Columbia.

Eight years of trying to climb one rung. His hands were calloused; he often thought of quitting. But he always remembered that he was trying to set himself up as a symbol of what a deaf person can do.

Midway, he came to Minnesota as coordinator of clinical services for the deaf at the State Public Welfare Department. That was in 1973. From that vantage, he hoped to achieve a marriage between the business-government sector and the hearing impaired people.

"Alas," he said, "it has not been all that I had hoped. Minnesota is far and away ahead of many other states, but we still discriminate against hearing-impaired citizens. We need more interpreters, many more. We need more interpreter training courses like that at St. Paul TVI.

"The concept of mainstreaming deaf people means that you no longer hire deaf people as their teachers. I point out to you a high school in the Twin Cities with fifty hearing-impaired students and not one deaf teacher or staff worker working with these children. What do hearing people know?"

When, in 1977, he was offered the chance to "cross the freeway" to St. Paul Ramsey as assistant director and therapist of the hospital center's mental health program for deaf persons, he leaped.

But as we spoke that afternoon in January, Dr. Chough was packing again. He would take along the Courage Center Phillips Award plaque he was given in 1978 and the Sertoma Club of St. Paul award for work well done on behalf of the people who can't hear. He would take his diplomas and certificates of excellence and pioneering.

These are now hanging on walls in his office in Michigan.

Nancy and their two children, Abby and Alex, who can hear, but have learned to ''speak'' in sign language, are with him on the next rung of the ladder.

How high will it go? How many more rungs are there left to climb?

Dr. Steven Chough shrugs, smiles and shakes his head. He doesn't know.

There will be as many as he has the courage to try reaching.

WILLIAM H. DEPARCQ

by

Daniel Huff

One June day in 1923, young Bill DeParcq lay seriously injured in a ditch near a Minnesota back country dirt road. He had hitched a ride from Staples, Minnesota, on his way to Canada's Lake Winnipeg, where he had planned to work as a guide that summer. But the Model A he was riding in jackknifed out of a rut in the road and flipped, sending him through the canvas roof. When he landed in the ditch, he broke his back.

William H. DeParcq had been born in New Orleans, March 27, 1905. He was two years old when his family moved to Minneapolis where Bill's father operated the Merchants Hotel. During World War I, the senior De Parcq saw another opportunity in hotel management and took over the National Hotel in Staples, Minnesota. This is how young Bill came to be living in northern Minnesota.

Now, at age eighteen, Bill had been looking forward to a couple of months of hunting and fishing. But all he could do was lie quietly as the uninjured driver of the Model A walked along the train tracks, back to the town of Thief River Falls for help. It was an extremely unpleasant wait. There was a terrific pain in his back, which he tried not to think about. He thought he must be dying, and, as the doctor confirmed later, he was very close.

He considered briefly the possibility that he might be paralyzed. In 1923, paraplegics generally did not live long, and their deaths were painful due to the inevitable bed sores and infections in that era before wonder drugs. That possibility was just too horrifying to contemplate there in the ditch as he realized he couldn't move a single muscle.

"I didn't find out until late that night that I had severed my spinal cord," he recalled. And when doctors told him he would be paralyzed from the waist down for the rest of his life, the young man was devastated.

He would not exactly call it a blessing in disguise, but distinguished retired attorney William DeParcq, looking back now, at the age of seventy-five, admits that he was able to help a lot of people, many of them paraplegics like himself, after the accident that altered his life.

"William H. DeParcq, attorney for the Plaintiff." In the 1940s and 1950s, lawyers all across the Midwest got nervous when they saw those words on the legal complaints they received on behalf of their large corporate clients. And with good reason: it generally meant they were about to lose a case.

"During his career as a personal injury attorney," said one of DeParcq's former partners, "Bill won millions of dollars for his clients. He was the first attorney ever to win a verdict in excess of $100,000 in a personal injury case. And that was in the days when a dollar was worth a good deal more than it is today."

He routinely won large settlements for the victims of industrial accidents or their survivors. And he never took the company's side against the little guy.

"There was absolutely no way I was ever going to do that after what I had been through," DeParcq said.

After a risky operation to save his life, one of the first laminectomies ever performed, a thoroughly dispirited young Bill lay in the Thief River Falls Hospital as bed sores literally ate into his bones.

"The hospital staff didn't expect him to live," said Billie Stine, who has been DeParcq's nurse for the past twenty-two years. "They were afraid to move him."

After months of watching her only child suffer, his anguished mother brought him home from the hospital and started him down the sometimes painful path to a useful life. She took him to the family's lakeside cottage near Motley, Minnesota. There, grasping the ceiling rafters for support, and with the constant encouragement and devotion of his parents, Bill learned to walk again.

"Actually," recalled his longtime friend and private investigator Bill Lehmeyer, "Bill couldn't exactly walk. He had these huge braces he'd slap on his legs, and then with a pair of crutches he could swing himself along. We traveled all over the country trying cases, and he'd never take a wheelchair. He'd use the crutches even if it was six blocks from the train to the hotel. That took real guts. Back then I can't remember another paraplegic who did that." In fact, DeParcq did not even own a wheelchair until after he was sixty years old.

Call it what you will, young Bill's confidence was restored when he enrolled in William Mitchell College of Law in St. Paul. His loyal mother sat through every class with him, helping him take notes. Outside of class she would walk with him so that he could get his exercise, reading to him from law books as they walked. When he graduated summa cum laude, the school gave her an honorable mention.

He was hired by a Minneapolis attorney. With Bill's ferocious appetite for work and with help from his mother, he built one of the most successful practices in town.

"He had two personal secretaries," recollected Bill Lehmeyer. "One to work the first shift and one for the second. Fourteen and twenty-hour days were common for him. He had one office in Minneapolis and another in Chicago.

"Bill threw himself completely into his work," continued Lehmeyer. "In many, many cases he altered his fee agreement so that he could give his injured and paralyzed clients extra money."

Wherever DeParcq went, Lehmeyer recalled, he would make a

point of stopping by a hospital or nursing home to chat with the paraplegics and encourage them to get up and start moving around. Eventually he became one of the first paraplegics to drive his own specially-modified car, which required a great deal of strength in the hands and arms in those days before power steering and power brakes.

While DeParcq was trying a case in Oklahoma, a federal judge asked him to talk to a young man who had been paralyzed in an accident and become severely depressed. "The boy was so impressed with Bill's visit," said a friend, "that he went through law school himself and eventually became a state supreme court justice."

"We'd fly thousands of miles out of our way to help paraplegics," Lehmeyer said. "In those days so many of them would go on self-pity binges. If Bill ever had that problem I never noticed it." Frequently, in his travels around the country, DeParcq would lecture to students or to various law groups.

According to his friends, DeParcq had a close relationship with another prominent American who lived with a disability: Franklin Delano Roosevelt. They met in 1936 when Roosevelt was campaigning for his second presidential term and DeParcq was running for a second term in Congress. "Roosevelt carried every Democrat in the nation into office except me!" DeParcq laughed. In those days the two men even looked alike, friends said, and they wrote to each other.

"Bill would light up a room when he entered," remembered former partner Norm Perl. "He had great flashing eyes and he loved to have fun. He worked hard and he played hard."

Despite his disability, DeParcq was an avid sportsman. "He'd go duck hunting in a blind," said a friend, "or we'd tie him onto the tailgate of a station wagon and prowl the corn fields during pheasant season." Pheasant hunting in South Dakota was an annual adventure.

Stine reports that DeParcq has always been an eager fisherman and an excellent swimmer. Once while fishing from a schooner twenty-five miles out in the Caribbean, DeParcq and some com-

Opposite: Sportsman DeParcq and Nurse Billie Stine with big catch

panions caught forty-two fish inside of an hour. Then a fierce tropical storm developed and the captain headed posthaste for port.

The schooner promptly arrived at the concrete dock, but, in DeParcq's own words, "Boat and concrete banged together with such fury that the captain feared I would be crushed between the dock and the vessel if an attempt was made to move me ashore.

"When the captain found out that I was a good swimmer, he instructed my nurse to get my bathing suit, which I quickly donned, and my nurse helped me discard my braces. Meanwhile, the captain moved the schooner about one thousand feet into the bay, and I was dumped into the water. A young Jamaican lad jumped in beside me and the two of us swam to shore. When we reached the shoreline, the lad lifted me out of the water and carried me ashore."

Nurse Billie Stine comments, "He traveled all over the world. We celebrated his sixtieth birthday in Hong Kong, and we visited Lebanon and Egypt in 1966, just a year before the Arab-Israeli War. He worked so hard that he had to get completely away at least once a year."

Other travels have included his three Caribbean cruises, a trip around the world on the Rotterdam, a cruise to the South Pacific islands, a visit to the Orient, travel to Europe on two occasions, yearly fishing trips to Canada and an especially memorable fishing expedition above the Arctic Circle.

DeParcq refers to the latter as, "The greatest fishing trip I ever took, to Great Bear Lake in the Northwest Territory of Canada, a hundred miles above the Arctic Circle. We flew in by plane from Winnipeg, stopping at Yellowknife. On the American continent, Great Bear Lake is second in size only to Lake Superior and is ice-free from the first week in June to the first week of September. The action was plentiful, including lake trout, silver trout, Arctic char, graylings and northerns."

DeParcq's comfortable lodge near Grand Rapids, Minnesota, has been another source of relaxation and pleasure. It was equipped with a seventy-foot outdoor lift running from the house to the dock. There was also his well-equipped houseboat, capable of sleeping six people.

It must be emphasized that DeParcq's interests have always included the needs of other people. He helped lay the groundwork for Courage Foundation and was a charter member. Courage Center has acknowledged his dedication by naming him an honorary life member of the Foundation.

In 1973, DeParcq retired from his law office. Since October of that year he has made his home in Tucson, Arizona. He suffered a severe stroke in June, 1974, but he has achieved ninety percent recovery.

Who would have thought, on that earlier June day back in 1923, that young Bill DeParcq, lying hopelessly paralyzed in a ditch at the side of a country road, would live so long and well. Who could have imagined that he would become, in the words of former partner Norm Perl, ". . . the finest personal injury attorney the state of Minnesota has ever produced. In his prime he was one of the top ten trial attorneys in the country."

The striken young man, for whom all but his mother had at one time abandoned hope, became dean of the prestigious International Academy of Trial Lawyers and appeared twice before the United States Supreme Court.

"He's the most terrific man I've ever known," says Lehmeyer. "His compassion, his skill and above all his fortitude in the face of tremendous adversity are beyond most people's comprehension."

HENRY W. HAVERSTOCK, JR.

by

Robert T. Smith

It was a Sunday in the autumn of 1939. For some reason it happened a lot during the fall of the year.

Henry W. Haverstock, Jr., then an active seventeen-year-old youth who played sandlot football and pole vaulted and, with his father, hunted and fished, was putting a golf ball in his back yard. He had dug holes in the lawn, and was having fun trying to get the white ball into them. At one point, he knelt down to retrieve the ball from a hole. He could not get up, at least not without help.

The incident came almost without warning. The previous day, however, he had awakened with a rather severe pain in his back and the back of his head. It had lasted about three hours, then had disappeared.

With effort, Henry finally got up from a kneeling to a standing position at his makeshift golf course, and continued the game. But he became weaker and weaker. With the aid of a brother, he made it inside the house to a couch. Then, again with help, he went to his bed. There he stayed for five months.

Henry, born in Minneapolis in 1922, went to Burroughs Elementary School, Ramsey Junior High and then Washburn Senior High School.

His lawyer father, a strong-minded but loving man, taught his son many things. Particularly, he taught young Henry that you do not give up, no matter what the adversity. The idea was to take problems and turn them into assets.

Young Henry had a normal childhood. He loved to be outdoors, to run and laugh and feel the strength mounting in his growing body. He believed, as most children do, that he was invincible, and immortal and that nothing bad could happen to him. And nothing untoward did happen to him until that autumn day in 1939.

After going from the couch to his bed, young Henry began to feel heavy pain. It affected his legs and abdomen and back and his arms and hands. In the first week, his temperature got as high as 104 degrees. For three weeks, he could not move without agonizing pain. "So great was the pain," he remembers, "that all wrinkles in the sheets and buttons on the mattress had to be removed before I felt in the least degree comfortable."

For six weeks, he had no treatment. No one seemed to know for sure what he had, for at that time not much was known about polio. They even called it by a different name: infantile paralysis. It is a disease of the nerves, and it probably was best that during the first weeks of pain, Henry did not know what hit him.

After the first six weeks, treatment began. The seventeen-year-old wasn't bitter about his affliction. He figured he would give it a good fight. He began strenuous exercise and massage. He used a four-wheeled walker — a metal-framed cart with a seat in the center. He sat on it and made it go with his legs. He invented exercises on that cart, movements for his legs, back and abdominal muscles.

The exercises and massage treatments kept him busy from 10 a.m. to 8 p.m. He operated a rig consisting of a wooden board three-and-a-half feet long, with a roller skate on each end. "I would lie on my side with one leg on the skate rig, and move my leg back and forth as the rig rolled on a large table leaf,'' Haverstock remembers.

There were three hospital stays, and he wore full-length leg braces from February to June, 1940. There was some improvement. But that could well have been normal improvement noticed by many polio victims in the early months of the disease. It might have happened without the exercises and massages and casts.

It was Haverstock's senior year at Washburn when he contracted polio. He was the only kid in his class who got it, and he had to graduate in a wheelchair. But he did not seek pity and was rewarded in kind by his fellow students — they did not offer any pity. It was about this time that Haverstock learned to use his head more than most of his friends. ''Thinking became my hobby.''

In February, 1940, he traveled to Warm Springs, Georgia, the favorite spa of President Franklin Delano Roosevelt, himself a polio victim. ''Warm Springs was beautiful. The buildings were pillared and white, and surrounded by rich green lawns.'' The medical staff at Warm Springs fitted Haverstock for braces — full-length leg splints, a body brace, even a thumb splint. He was put to bed for four months, getting out only once in the morning for exercise in the special pool and a light massage.

But instead of concentrating on the muscles which might make him walk again, the staff members had a coordinated muscle program. He could use other muscles to help his legs move. ''In short, it was a failure,'' says Haverstock. ''The muscles which should have been strengthened were weak, and gradually wasting away. The braces plus a body cast, served to stiffen my legs and torso.''

After several weeks he was permitted to sit in a wheelchair for fifteen minutes a day, then twenty, then twenty-five. Finally, he was allowed to wheel himself around the complex at will.

He left Warm Springs June 3, 1940, a somewhat dejected youth. Among the last things they told him were: ''No victim of polio who has paralysis ever regains full use of his muscles. You, Henry, will never be able to walk.'' They did not know

Haverstock very well. "I have never thought of myself as a cripple."

His father drove him home from Georgia. Young Haverstock lay on a stretcher settled across the two car seats. On the way, his father talked to him about how there would be no such thing as quitting the fight against the disease. When they arrived home, Henry was put to bed in his leg braces and body cast. He was not, of course, able to stand or walk.

Then came Sister Elizabeth Kenny. The tough, outspoken backlander from Australia, who bullied doctors and snorted at the then-current treatments for polio, became the means for a young high school graduate to realize his goal. Haverstock became Sister Kenny's first regular patient in this country. When the formidable woman originally met with the young man, she said, "You'll walk."

"I believed her," said Haverstock. Then Sister Kenny looked him over, and ordered the braces off. "I never want to see them again."

Haverstock remembers well that first encounter with the remarkable woman: "My feeling toward her as she slowly stepped into my bedroom at home was one of awe and respect. She bore herself erectly. Her appearance was that of one who had been called upon to shoulder all the troubles of a war-torn world. Her face was serious and she looked deeply thoughtful. I greeted her with a cheerful 'Good morning,' which she promptly returned."

Henry's father carried him downstairs and placed him on the dining room table, at Sister Kenny's request. She then examined Haverstock more carefuly. With a bit of humor, Haverstock comments, "I then knew where the phrase, she was 'Peck-peck-pecking all around' originated in the popular 1940 song hit."

There followed the famous Kenny treatment, which included training him to know the location and function of his various muscles. A year later, young Haverstock was walking with the aid of crutches. "The nurses couldn't believe their eyes," he remembers.

With his crutches and his sense of humor, Haverstock began

life in a world designed for the non-handicapped. The world came in second.

He entered the University of Minnesota and discovered that, for some perverse reason, most of his classes were on upper floors. He made the stairs daily by keeping close to the walls. "And the steps outside the buildings were a terror, particularly in the winter." With the help of special equipment, he could drive a car, which made his life more comfortable.

As in high school, the University students did not cause Haverstock any trouble. No pity or teasing. "I had help, if anything." But he became somewhat of a loner. It helped with his contemplation, aided in the development of his thinking process. "I found being somewhat of a loner a virtue," he says. "I did not mind being a majority of one."

Haverstock graduated from the University in 1945 and went to the University of Southern California, where a year later he received a law degree. Then began an impressive career in law and service to his community, and a full life as a husband and father. The following are just some of his activities and accomplishments:

First chairman, Architectural Barriers Committee of the Minnesota Society for Crippled Children and Adults, now Courage Center; chairman, Minnesota State Bar Association Special Committee to codify and redraft the Minnesota State Criminal Code; chairman four years and director twenty-two years, of the Minneapolis Downtown YMCA; past president, Metropolitan YMCA Men's Club; past president, Minneapolis Downtown Exchange Club.

Selected by *Time* Magazine and the Minneapolis Chamber of Commerce as one of 100 Outstanding Young Men in 1953.

Past chairman, Minnesota State Bar Association committee which created the KSTP-Radio series, "You and the Law;" former instructor, William Mitchell College of Law; for twenty years a member of the speakers bureau of the Community Chest, now the United Way.

Politically, this "handicapped" man has been very active. He was a delegate to many county and state Republican conventions in Minnesota, and was formerly chairman of the research committee of the Hennepin County Young Republican League. In 1956, he ran, unsuccessfully, for the Republican nomination for Minnesota attorney general.

Haverstock has worked long and hard to improve things for the handicapped in Minnesota. Besides serving on the board of Courage Center for many years, he has spent time lobbying with local and state governments.

With his help, Minnesota became one of the first states in the nation to adopt a comprehensive legal code requiring such things as ramps and slanted curbing for those in wheelchairs. "People should spend a day in a wheelchair," said Haverstock. "Then we'd get a lot of action."

He considers the Minneapolis Skyway system a model of architecture for the handicapped. Referring to the Investors' Diversified Services Company, he says, "We got IDS to spend $40,000 just to eliminate four steps to the Skyway. It's a ramp now."

Not everything has gone well, though. Haverstock is perplexed by one Minneapolis area shopping center. Wanting to do things right in terms of the handicapped, the center's designers put ramps in everywhere. "Then they constructed a raised, decorative section between the handicapped parking spaces and the front door. It had curbs all around it, hindering wheelchair access."

Haverstock was married to his first wife, Jean, in 1950. They had three children, Henry W. III; William W. "Bill;" and Alice. Jean died at age forty-nine of cancer. In 1970, Haverstock married his present wife, Shirley, who has one daughter, Patrice.

In recent years, aside from his Minneapolis law practice, Haverstock has had a "hobby": real estate. He has bought more than fifty properties, including office and apartment buildings and farm land. He is now working on a book about his real estate dealings entitled, "Wealth From a Wheelchair."

The "wheelchair" of that title reflects his life since 1977. He walked with only the crutches for thirty-seven years, but it took

Opposite: The young Haverstock

its toll on his knees. The knee muscles finally gave out, and he now gets around in a wheelchair. But even in that he finds good. "With the crutches, I used to be terrified by winter icy conditions. I'm not at all worried now in a wheelchair."

When he is not in court or making a real estate deal or working for some community cause, Haverstock indulges in his hobbies: wood carving, rug hooking, stamp collecting and traveling. "We've gone just about everywhere, including a trip around the world." And he reads, everything from the *Wall Street Journal* to non-fiction books such as *Future Shock*.

Haverstock has used his sense of humor well to help him in life. He can tell jokes or relate humorous experiences he has had. Part of it is to get by situations involving people who are uncomfortable around the handicapped.

"I like to talk to people, at parties and such. But some ignore you if you are in a wheelchair. I've gotten used to it, but sometimes it makes me angry. It bothers me that people can't deal with realities."

And Haverstock has another little pet peeve. Some people tend to hover over him when conversing. "It gives you the feeling people are looking down at you." It is better when they sit down and the person in a wheelchair can look them in the face instead of at their stomachs.

Then there are those who think, if you are in a wheelchair, you are mentally deficient. Haverstock, for instance, is not pleased when waiters or waitresses automatically hand the bill to his wife.

And what is the philosophy of this man who was cut down by polio at the age of seventeen?

First of all, he agrees with Abraham Lincoln: "You are as happy as you make up your mind to be." Nothing magical from the outside is going to make you happy, if you have made up your mind to be bitter.

Is he better off because he had polio? He thinks so. "Without the experiences that came with polio, I think I would not have developed as much mentally. I'd have made a living, I guess, but maybe not have done as many things in life."

As he says, thinking is his main hobby. "I like to puzzle things out." And he's not past oriented, as he claims ninety-five per cent of people are. "I like to know where I am going and how to use what I know to get there. The hard part is to figure out where one wants to go.

"Too many people are shackled with rigidities and complexes. . . . We need flexibility in life.

"A lot of people are stuck in the mud, going nowhere fast."

But not Henry W. Haverstock, Jr., whose only crutches in life were made in Canada.

GEORGE "JUDD" JACOBSON

by

Pauline Walle

Comedian Jack Benny had just presented a concert in Rochester, Minnesota — complete with violin solos — and was speaking at a private party in his honor. He paused in the middle of his remarks, reminded of an incident earlier that day in 1965.

A radio newsman had wanted to tape a conversation with Benny. Since the reporter was a quadriplegic confined to a wheelchair, Benny had suggested a private session where concert and cocktail crowds would not close in. "As you know I've been interviewed by a lot of people during my career," the actor told his audience. "But that young man from Owatonna . . . that was the best interview I've ever had."

The young man was George "Judd" Jacobson. Today, the fifty-two-year-old Jacobson is making his own news from a sophisticated home studio. He is also making waves with an international travel service for the handicapped.

Jacobson grew up in Owatonna where he was a first-string athlete in football and wrestling. He lettered as a high school sophomore. Hopes for a continued sports career snapped when he was the victim of a diving accident in a local gravel pit. It left Judd Jacobson paralyzed at sixteen.

"At first I thought I could handle it, but it got more traumatic as it went on," he recalls. "Rehabilitation wasn't as fast as I'd expected. I lay in the Owatonna Hospital for a year and a half."

He could not be treated by Mayo Clinic personnel right away because it was wartime and there was a shortage of doctors and nurses in nearby Rochester, too. Doctors' wives were doing a lot of the floor duty, supervised by nurses.

Finally, a Clinic specialist wrote Jacobson's parents that they could accept Judd in a rehabilitation program. He spent another year and a half in Rochester hospitals, responding to physical therapy. He began to learn to use what little musculature remained in his arms.

Jacobson went home to Owatonna. He was still "flat on his back," selling magazines from his bed when a friend of his introduced the subject of radio. Or re-introduced it, because as a 4-H member, Judd had done some broadcasts with radio-ad man Walter Bruzek. "I'd heard Judd could do some typing and figured he could help keep Rochester's KROC station in Owatonna alive," said Bruzek.

Jacobson maintained the satellite station until KROC withdrew it five years later. KDHL in Faribault put a similar station in Owatonna, and "I was their radio," said Jacobson, who worked those call letters for the next twenty-five years. In the past couple of years he has been with KOWO, Waseca. All of this broadcasting has been remote from the home he built in Owatonna.

In the early years of his recovery, Jacobson lived with his family and considered that home a halfway house where he got a lot of support for the future. "While I was hospitalized I watched some $100,000 rehabilitation jobs go right into nursing homes," he said. "I was fortunate to have a place where I could get my act together and decide what I wanted to do."

With the help of his contractor father and a Wayzata designer, Jacobson planned his cozy, contemporary rambler. Laid out as side-by-side apartments with a common kitchen, it allowed for live-in attendant care. It was outfitted with lifts over bed and tub and had an intercom that a quadriplegic could handle. The house was so attractive it was featured widely by the media. Two thousand letters came from as far away as South America and Europe, from people who wanted to adapt its features to their own handicaps.

But Jacobson did not need the attendant care much longer. Branching out in his work with KDHL, he had begun to travel and had escorted several tours for the station. He was conducting a Hawaiian trip for forty-five able-bodied people when he met his future wife, Barbara Williams of Chester, England. She was a ticket manager for Trans-World Airlines in Honolulu.

"I was in my late twenties and had done a lot of things," said Barbara. "I guess I was looking for something a little different — a challenge. Judd asked me to dinner. He was someone I really could communicate with. He was persistent, and the relationship progressed." Her travel passes turned into several visits in the states, and they were married in 1969 at a Methodist church in Owatonna.

Barbara cheerfully took over Judd's nursing and personal care. He cannot dress, undress, or even roll over in bed unassisted. Once he is in his chair he can shave, wash, feed himself and work at the desk in his office.

He is surrounded by a complete remote broadcasting system, tape recorders, mixers and microphones. He does three programs a day Monday through Saturday. "The most important thing we broadcast here is the same as it has been the last ten years — change," said Jacobson. "Growth. Industry is dynamic in Owatonna." With the help of a van and driver he covers council meetings, press conferences and dinner speeches in and out of town.

During his radio days Jacobson also followed the career of First District Congressman, and now Governor, Albert Quie. Quie is still a good family friend. Also, Jacobson was spokesman for a handicapped group that met with former President Gerald Ford at the White House.

"He didn't use notes. He was eloquent. And Ford really listened," said Barbara. "But whether it's President Ford or Governor Quie or some farm kids at a convention, Judd is stimulating during an interview. He asks the right questions and puts people at ease."

Since Barbara wanted to keep up her profession, she runs a downtown office devoted to the tour industry Jacobson started and manages Flying Wheels, the agency specifically geared to getting handicapped people on vacation. The agency once booked a disabled couple on a Hawaiian honeymoon.

The Jacobsons complement each other in the business. "Judd's a tiger so he sells the advertising. We have a good volume and he's the one who got it. But he's a disaster when it comes to detail so I handle the office and finances."

The couple fly ahead and check the accessibility of planes, hotels, restaurants and passenger vehicles before they take a group on tour. Flying Wheels is international now, with the largest commercial services for handicapped travel. It books about 200 people annually on ten trips to places like Hawaii, Scandinavia, Jamaica and aboard the Queen Elizabeth II. There also are numerous single tours.

As if that were not enough to keep busy, Jacobson also runs Judd Medical Supply. Wheelchairs, walkers and hospital beds are rented or sold to people in southeastern Minnesota. He keeps the books nights and Sundays.

Does he overdo it, maybe try too hard to prove himself? Judd looked out the window of his home office one recent Sunday afternoon and considered the question. "I suppose I look out on a beautiful day, and when I can't be playing golf or football the only answer is work," Jacobson said. "I do it seven days a week."

"I consider myself severely handicapped — a high quad — and I'm daily aware of that fact. It's been thirty-six years." While Jacobson does not let himself brood too long, he is aware that it took a lot of help along the way. He lists the "credits" for his lifestyle.

"I'm highly dependent upon other people. I couldn't have suc-

ceeded without my parents and sisters, people like Walt Bruzek, support from this community." Besides her company as wife and business partner, "Barbara provides a great deal of my daily nursing care. It's less demanding than having a live-in attendant." And then he smiles, "And a lot more fun!" Jacobson also depends on a full-time attendant from Pillsbury Bible College nearby and a high school junior to drive him to his various appointments.

The active quad has won a number of awards for his courage. He especially is proud of having been Handicapped Minnesotan of the Year in 1965 because, "I was just beginning to feel financially independent and was doing things on my own." Judd was also a recipient of the Rose and Jay Phillips Award presented by Courage Center in 1967.

He has been a "mover" for accessibility statewide, serving on boards and committees as one way to "get the message across to able-bodied people who I think need my perspective." He serves on the Board of Directors of the Sister Kenny Institute, the Minnesota State Council for the Handicapped, and Courage Center. He was an early member of the Courage Center Architectural Barriers program which did so much to help provide greater accessibility for wheelchair users in Minnesota, and a member of the National Advisory Committee for an Accessible Environment.

"I tell people there are many major opportunities available to the severely handicapped," Jacobson says. "But they can't realize them until the barriers are removed. They also need a great deal of support from their families. If they try to do it alone, it's nearly impossible."

While there would not seem to be a spare hour in the Jacobsons' existence, both enjoy sports and may go off to a game on a weekend. Barbara was in Bloomington one Saturday while Judd worked in the office. The phone rang — their state line — and it was Barbara calling to say, "Did you see that!" He had been talking with a visitor and had missed the play on the television set nearby.

She also had called just to check on him and "to be sure he wasn't lonesome."

Barbara Jacobson reflected on her husband's courage. "He's persistent and dynamic," she said. "That's why Judd's here today."

LINDA MARZINSKE

by

Jane Rachner

Escape comes in three varieties. There is head-in-the-sand escape, the purpose of which is to avoid facing facts. There is cop-out escape, the purpose of which is to shun duties and responsibilities. Finally, there is heroic escape, the purpose of which is to break the chains of limitations in order to fulfill a destiny.

Only the third variety applies to Linda Marzinske. Since early childhood she has fought diligently against the helplessness that could have resulted from a congenital misfortune. Linda came into the world with only one leg and only the upper portions of her two arms.

Linda was the Marzinskes' first child. The doctor at Brainerd Hospital called her a triple amputee. He gave her parents a choice: they could give her up, if they wished. Linda's parents would not hear of such a thing.

The only one of the Marzinske children born with a physical disability, Linda was always treated just like the other children.

Linda's parents, confident of the probability that Linda will out-live them, made it their goal to help her achieve independence so that she would not have to spend her life in an institution.

Linda's parents knew just about everyone in the small town of Calumet, Minnesota, where she was born, including the principal of the elementary school. Linda still vividly remembers the day early in her childhood when her mother proudly took her to the elementary school where the principal asked her to demonstrate that she could color, paste, and even print her name. Without delay, the principal introduced her to the kindergarten teacher, and Linda's formal education had begun.

"The teacher was a woman just out of school, taking her first job, and she was eager for the challenge of teaching me," says Linda. "Her name was Miss Bell, and I still remember that she was always ready to help me when I needed her but never did more for me than I wanted her to."

Thanks to Linda's successful start in Calumet there was no problem with her entering first grade after the family moved to Albert Lea. Linda had proved she was able to compete with other children her age, and throughout her schooling she was "mainstreamed," as the expression goes today. She never had to attend a special class because of her disability.

While Linda was growing up, it was her family's practice not to coddle her. Her brother and sister always found some way to include her on outings, even if they had to carry her. Her parents were not embarrassed if Linda spilled her food at a restaurant. If she stumbled and fell with her artificial leg, they would calmly let her get up by herself.

Another example of the kind of independence Linda's parents helped her to develop is the mobility that comes with driving a car. Her father taught her to drive the family car. Later, when she bought a car of her own, her father custom-fitted it with a special knob on the steering wheel. The knob has a ring into which Linda can fit the single digit she possesses on her short left arm. Her father also equipped the dashboard with extra long knobs for heater, defroster, windshield wipers, and lights.

Now, after fifteen years of driving, Linda's record is unblemished by so much as a parking ticket or a dented fender, and this should bring a blush of mortification to the insurance company who initially labeled her "high risk."

Inevitably Linda felt frustrations during her teens, years that typically bring feelings of awkwardness even to agile youngsters. Linda found that triple amputees are not likely to be invited on dates, or to the prom.

In many respects, college was an improvement over high school. Being more mature, college students place less emphasis on physical attributes and give more credit for wit and intelligence.

Linda thought carefully before deciding on a college. The choice was not made any easier by well-meaning friends who bluntly expressed their opinion that Linda would not possibly be able to cope with college life.

Undaunted, Linda and her family looked into various campuses. They chose the University of Minnesota at Morris, partly because it was built around a mall with everything in easy walking distance of the dormitories and no hills that would be difficult for Linda to negotiate with her artificial leg.

In her usual manner of understating all difficulties, Linda claims that she managed the four years with only such slight traumas as having to be picked out of a snowbank when she fell occasionally. After earning her bachelor's degree with a major in public speaking, Linda attended Brown Institute in Minneapolis, where she studied radio and television broadcasting. With her training, Linda obtained a position in the public relations department of Courage Center, and held it for five years. During all her years of participation in Courage Center programs, first as a camper and then as a staff member, she was a tremendous inspiration and symbol of courage to those who knew her.

While in that position she was asked to be part of the speaker's bureau of the United Way. This led directly to her first meeting with Oren McDonald, a vice president at Prudential Insurance Company where Linda now works.

As Senior Education Specialist in Prudential's Employee Development Division, Linda encourages new employees to be aware of the strengths and weaknesses each one brings to his or her new job. She realizes that people who believe they have no weaknesses are not likely to do a good job of surmounting them. Unrecognized disabilities will reduce people's value to the company more than the disabilities of employees who understand themselves realistically.

Linda orients new employees, teaches Customer Service, Four-Step Method of Job Instruction, and Career Orientation, and coordinates registration for self-study courses available to employees on all aspects of the insurance business.

Now that she is working for Prudential, Linda still keeps her commitment to the United Way. During the 1979 campaign she gave a total of some thirty talks. In recognition of her efforts, Linda was one of the 1979 recipients of the Rose and Jay Phillips Awards bestowed annually by Courage Center for outstanding employee service performed in spite of severe physical limitations.

In addition to her full-time position at Prudential and her United Way activities, Linda keeps her spacious apartment sparkling clean and neat without relying upon the dozen servants that most people enjoy — ten facile fingers and two full-length arms. Except for a couple of times a year when Linda lets her mother help with the spring and fall cleaning, she remains completely independent as a homemaker.

If she is complimented on the remarkableness of this dual achievement of holding a responsible position in a large company and keeping control of her environment and her daily life, Linda will accept the praise graciously and then add modestly, "But I'm not alone in having problems to overcome. In fact, everyone has disabilities."

A lifetime of awareness of her physical limitations has made Linda realize how unimportant is a person's outward appearance by comparison with the heart and mind within. Not that Linda neglects her health or personal appearance. Her hair glistens from

Opposite: Marzinske on the job at Courage Center

the daily shampoos that she manages by herself, and her personality is enhanced by her clear skin, her even, white teeth and her delicately chiseled facial features.

Still, when people see a disability like Linda's, which they know they could not handle with a fraction of her aplomb, they often find themselves being overtaken by feelings of guilt. Linda understands these reactions and goes out of her way to put people at ease when she sees that well-meant pity has made people awkward in her presence.

For instance, one day at Southdale Shopping Center a preschooler hanging on his mother's arm caught sight of Linda and said loudly, "Look, that lady broke both her arms." The mother shushed the child and snatched him away in embarrassment.

But Linda gave the woman a friendly smile and said she did not mind the boy's curiosity. She explained to the child that having had the misfortune to be born with short arms and no hands, she had nevertheless learned to do many things well.

Linda prefers to handle curiosity openly lest children otherwise learn hurtful habits of avoidance and rejection toward people with obvious defects. Instead of feeling irritated with people who lack poise when they meet her for the first time, she merely takes mental note of their reaction, thus gaining an understanding of human nature that a psychologist might envy.

Linda's attitude more often inspires people she meets. That's why things happen to Linda that do not happen to other people. A few years ago while on a plane flight to a convention in another city, Linda had a chance conversation with a man sitting next to her. She told him about the convention and casually mentioned the name of the hotel at which it would be held. A couple of hours later, Linda answered the bellboy's knock at the door of her hotel room and was handed, to her surprise, a dozen long-stemmed roses. The card with them revealed that they were from the airplane acquaintance. He wrote that he wanted to pay tribute to her exceptional personality.

Linda likes to travel whenever she can, and does not allow her disability to hamper her plans. Her vacation trips are active rather than passive. She can take only so much basking in the sun before her intellectual curiosity gets her moving. Linda is not one to pamper herself. On a recent trip her traveling companion was another young woman born without arms. The friend, having achieved less independence in dressing herself, needed help from Linda each day.

It is easy to see that Linda is an activist, conscious of her membership in the disabled community and loyal to the needs of that group. But she keeps her contacts with people as broad and varied as possible. Current best-sellers, movies, football, baseball and other sports events, plays, concerts and card games are some of the interests and pastimes Linda shares with her many able-bodied friends.

A good friend, Donna Warren, who works at Courage Center and met Linda there says, "Linda is more like a sister to me than just a friend. Because she's awfully good company, my two sons and I ask her to go places with us often, sometimes two or three times a week. Linda's the kind of person you can depend on for her good judgment. She's a very down-to-earth person. Yet she also seems to have a God-given charisma."

Comments Linda, "My faith is one thing that keeps me afloat," but she admits that also very important to her are her friends and relatives. Linda credits her family and friends with contributing to her miraculous achievement, and they give credit right back to Linda herself.

Linda deserves their admiration. She is a young woman who uses her charisma to help change the outlook of those escapists who refuse to face facts or who avoid encounters with the responsibilities of life. Escape from reality and escape from responsibility are isolationist reactions and are in sharp contrast with the philosophy of Linda Marzinske. In her own words, Linda is first and foremost, a "people person."

MAX RHEINBERGER

by

Janet S. Burns

"Max Rheinberger is a symbol of courage and hope for America's handicapped citizens. His life has been an answer to those who question whether America has what it takes to be a great nation." Those were Hubert Humphrey's words when Rheinberger received the Handicapped American of the Year award in 1968.

"I have a feeling that in this world there are two kinds of people — those who give more than they take and those who take more than they give. A person with my disability necessarily has to take a lot, so he has to give a lot." That is the philosophy the fifty-year-old Duluth business man has developed since he became a quadriplegic in 1952, when polio struck him down at the age of twenty-three. It is no happenstance that one sobriquet he earned (in a national business weekly) was that of one of the "Gutsiest Americans."

Rheinberger claims to have become a successful business executive because a person in his condition, "has to become an executive. He can't mow the lawn, dig ditches, or do all the manual kinds of things that exist." So he went about convincing those around him, and eventually the whole nation, that seriously disabled persons can live full and complete lives without any basic limitations on their potential.

Max Rheinberger's story is one of success in business, success in politics, success as a volunteer in a broad range of activities, and success as a man. He has been a resident of Duluth all his life. He was born December 11, 1929, to Max and Isabel Rheinberger, and educated in Duluth schools. Word gets around that he was something of a devil as a young man.

Polio struck while Rheinberger was working in the office of the Duluth, Mesabi and Iron Range Railway Company. "I don't think I was told by a doctor that I wouldn't be able to lead a normal life, and for a long period of time I thought I'd get back slowly or wake up some day and be perfect and it would all be a bad dream," Rheinberger recalls.

After three months in an iron lung and five more months in a Duluth hospital, Rheinberger was transferred to Sheltering Arms in Minneapolis, then a Sister Elizabeth Kenny type program aimed specifically at polio patients. After eighteen months, he was transferred back to Duluth, this time to St. Luke's Hospital Infirmary where he was told he was as rehabilitated as the medical community thought possible in those days.

They didn't know Max!

The Infirmary at that time, in Rheinberger's own words, was, "in effect where old people were sent to die." With one or two exceptions, he does not recall seeing anyone who was not bordering on senility. That fact alone spurred him on to try for a normal life outside.

"It's not in me to lay down and quit," Rheinberger says. A good deal of support at this time came from his father, Max Sr., who, according to the son, "was a big help and supplied lots of contacts."

The worst days of his convalescence, "if you could call it that," were those later days at Sheltering Arms when he realized he would never be a great deal better. He also remembers with mental pain the year following that realization, a year that remained without hope until he became involved in vocational rehabilitation. Rheinberger has been a rehabilitation booster ever since.

The prime mover in his recovery, Rheinberger freely admits, was A. W. "Gus" Gehrke, of the Minnesota Division of Vocational Rehabilitation. The DVR supplied Rheinberger with his motorized wheelchair, but most of the Duluth staff chided Gehrke when he arranged for Max to take a correspondence course in accounting, through the division. They did not regard the polio victim as a feasible employment commodity.

Gehrke has written, "Max was a real challenge to us. Every test had showed his high intelligence and talents. We felt it would be a crime if we could not help him put his talents to productive use. You see, it's a person's abilities that really count a lot more than his disabilities. But of course, we're quite realistic about this, too."

Teaching himself to type by manipulating a cigarette holder in his teeth, Rheinberger learned to type assignments, achieved high grades and completed a four-year course in two years.

Through polio, he had been deprived of the musculature in his legs, trunk and arms, with the exception of a trace in his left arm. To get maximum use of that arm, he relies upon an anti-gravity sling of his own design. It works on a helical spring principle with swinging weights.

Completely undaunted, Rheinberger now began a difficult but surprisingly fast comeback. He knew he wanted to work for an enterprise which emphasized performance rather than normality in arms and legs, so he started the business himself.

Office Services, Incorporated, which is still in operation, was set up to train and employ handicapped persons. The training of people with both physical and mental handicaps was underwritten by the rehabilitation division. During its nearly twenty-five years, the firm has helped hundreds of so-called unemployable individuals to become successful employees.

The business supplies stenographic and accounting services to local firms and has been staffed by handicapped persons who are in training for gainful employment. The staff also helps people with tax returns.

Meanwhile, Rheinberger found time for a personal life. After ten years of friendship, he and Marianne Hoiem were married in Lakeside Presbyterian Church in August, 1964. They have lived for many years in Duluth's first high-rise apartment building. Their comfortable two-bedroom apartment lends itself to the Rheinberger life style.

The man of the house says, "It's plenty large enough for us. A person can't really sleep in more than one bed, eat at more than one table or cook on more than one stove." The woman of the house will admit to having been Max's chief aide for many years.

It cost the State of Minnesota approximately $1,400 to rehabilitate Max Rheinberger, a sum which he repaid in taxes in 1957–58, only a year after the expense was incurred.

Gehrke and Rheinberger figured that the taxes generated by Max in the twenty years since rehabilitation, in income, property and personnel, almost exactly equalled the entire state budget for rehabilitation in the year 1957–58. That just proves, says Rheinberger, that a human service program can make a good return on an investment in people with handicaps.

Office Services was only the beginning. In rapid succession Rheinberger founded, operated and served as president of seven different businesses.

He originated Lee's Hospital Supply in 1959; Twin Ports Convalescent Service, Incorporated, in 1962; Northland Ambulance and First Street Properties in 1966; and Compudata in 1969. It was not until 1971 that he became owner and publisher of the St. Louis County *Financial Record* in Duluth.

Over the years Rheinberger did everything he could to employ people with disabilities.

Financial success brought him another sobriquet — "King Midas" — from some persons. But the "king" does not mind a bit. "I have done some things that have made some money, but it doesn't happen by accident."

"I don't think disabled persons are any different than anybody else — there are happy ones, sick ones, fat ones, skinny ones, and miserable ones, and I don't really think the disability makes anyone any less happy. I frankly think I'm a better and more complete person today than I would have been without the disability. I never thought I couldn't do it — why not? What did I have to lose?"

Rheinberger now considers himself partially retired. He and his wife spend three months — January to April — in Honolulu's sunshine. During the fall there are usually a few weeks in a southern setting. During the summer there are long weekends from Thursday afternoon until Monday at a lake home where both can soak up the northern Minnesota sun.

Rheinberger still manages Office Services. Twin Ports Transporation Service used to include both ambulances and school buses, but now it is down to buses. Rheinberger retains the presidency of Compudata and a computer store but is not particularly active. Basically, he says he is not involved in day-to-day activities. He is still the publisher of the *Financial Record.*

"My prime occupation," Rheinberger admits, "is no longer running businesses, but managing investments and doing some development work. I guess I have associates in all kinds of businesses. And I am also a partner in some real estate and recreational syndicates.

"The last three or four years I have tried to be involved in those things which have a social need . . . or provide the best return on my investment."

He has also pointed out that a time arrives when a man wonders why he is working so hard to make a record or pile up money.

"I've tried to take over one new project a year and do it successfully. So far I'm right on target. I've been fortunate to make enough money to become financially secure. There gets to be a point when you wonder why you're working so hard. I'm sure we all know people in businesses today who simply don't have to work but continue doing it. I don't intend to do that. They are killing themselves."

Rheinberger says his health has been excellent, and except for a short, two-day period, he has not occupied a hospital bed since his long-ago bout with polio. He has a routine physical once a year.

The blue-eyed, graying entrepreneur extraordinaire still wears the same size belt and shirt size as when he was nineteen. That in itself is a rather important accomplishment.

Not insignificant have been Rheinberger's ventures into politics. Elected in April, 1969, as an at-large member of the Duluth City Council, he became vice president and then president within months. He was re-elected for a second term and later served as chairman of the Council's finance committee.

Ben Boo, Duluth mayor during part of Rheinberger's term in office, said, "One never thought of Max as being disabled. He was so bright, so perceptive and had so much ability, that his handicap was not part of it at all. He traveled both physically and mentally right along with the council."

Henry Royer, who admits he got to know Rheinberger at their two meetings a week as city councilors, says, "I sat between him and another councilor and would pass on remarks. I grew close to him and was convinced his thought processes were super. I was confident of his ability."

In 1977 Rheinberger resigned to avoid a conflict of interest between his business and Council decisions.

During his tenure, he successfully sponsored legislation for the benefit of the handicapped, including a model ordinance on architectural barriers and civil service regulations that enable employment of the physically disabled and mentally retarded. Meanwhile he continued to work with national organizations to promote the same legislation.

He was also active politically in the Eighth Congressional District. First, as a Republican, he was one of six Minnesotans to receive the "Republicans Care" award in 1965. It was, in truth, a tribute to his work on behalf of people with handicaps. He has been general chairman of campaigns that elected an incumbent city councilor, two state legislators and a school board member — all on a non-partisan basis.

116

Then along came 1974 when, as an Independent, Rheinberger acted as finance director and manager of a campaign which elected United States Representative James Oberstar, Minnesota's Eighth District Democratic-Farmer-Labor Congressman.

Concurrently with his political participation, Rheinberger's volunteer activities were thriving.

Until about three years ago when the trips started to wind down, Rheinberger figured that he and his wife had logged 100,000 miles to numerous meetings and engagements to speak for people with handicaps. He was, by all reports, an effective, inspiring and dedicated spokesman for their programs. He would do three or four trips a year to Washington, D.C., and dozens each year to the Twin Cities area. Those traveling days have pretty well ceased for the semi-retired executive.

No organization for handicapped people was without Rheinberger's help. He has been treasurer, patients' service chairman and vice president of the Indianhead Chapter of the Muscular Dystrophy Association. He was a member of the board of the Duluth Rehabilitation Center for six years and was active in a capital fund drive to build a new facility.

For four years Rheinberger was on the Board of Directors of the Kenny Rehabilitation Institute, and he devoted one year to a committee directing a study for Duluth's Sheltered Workshop.

In 1974 he was made a member of the National Advisory Committee of the Handicapped for the United States Department of Health, Education and Welfare. His term has now expired. The committee had the responsibility for the special education programs for handicapped people, and acted as the board of regents for a number of federal colleges, including the National Technical Institute for the Deaf.

The Minnesota State Council for the Handicapped, which Rheinberger was a prime mover in establishing, has become a national example of consumer involvement and good planning. The Conference was a starting point for the legislation it sponsored, providing direct involvement in program planning to disabled persons.

Rheinberger serves on the President's Committee on Employment of the Handicapped and has been a member of its executive committee. This group played a large part in securing employment legislation which mandates that significant numbers of people with handicaps be involved in both planning and implementation. Rheinberger feels that his role in this endeavor has been his most important contribution to helping people with handicaps determine their own future.

One board in Duluth which still boasts of having him as a member is the United Day Activity Center for the Handicapped.

This is only a partial list.

All of this volunteer work has engendered many honors for Rheinberger.

As early as 1958 there was a citation for meritorious service from the President's Committee on Employment of the Handicapped. The next year Rheinberger was named Outstanding Young Man in Duluth; a year later he won the Free Enterprise Award for Duluth. In 1962 he was named one of Minnesota's Ten Outstanding Young Men and was the Minnesota nominee for the National Ten Outstanding Young Men.

He was a 1964 recipient of a Rose and Jay Phillips Award given to outstanding handicapped Minnesotans by Courage Center.

At the time of Rheinberger's being chosen Handicapped American of the Year, Hubert Humphrey reminded the audience that CBS newsman Eric Sevareid had introduced Rheinberger as an "extraordinary creature whose life exemplifies the indestructibility of the human spirit."

It was Humphrey who added that he considered it a "rare honor" to be from the same state as Rheinberger.

On that day, Rheinberger says, he felt a responsibility to the handicapped community because of the "recognizability, stature and credibility such an award brings. . . . When I accepted the award in Washington, I immediately called for better organization and more input of the handicapped community into the programs which were affecting their lives both at a volunteer and government level."

There is more.

Until he "outgrew" the organization, Rheinberger was an active member of the Duluth Jaycees and a director for eight years. During those years he was chairman of the Portorama, a now defunct annual civic celebration. For his work he has received three local and three state Jaycee awards.

In 1974 Rheinberger was chosen to serve on the Duluth Bicentennial Commission and was a member of its executive committee.

As a good businessman, Rheinberger has been a member of the Duluth Area Chamber of Commerce and active in its tourist and convention bureau; a charter member of the Duluth Civitan Club, a former member of the Duluth Art Institute board, a member of the executive board of the North Star Council of Boy Scouts and a very active promoter of Junior Achievement, the organization which teaches high school youths about the business world.

As an active member of the Lakeside Presbyterian Church, Rheinberger has served on its board of trustees and taught Sunday School.

Whatever he has given to the community — to the handicapped and to the physically able — Max Rheinberger is certainly not sorry that he did what he did. When asked if he ever felt like giving up somewhere along the road, he commented, "Who doesn't feel that way once in a while. Everybody has their ups and downs."

He certainly has never asked for special treatment. "I don't think you really achieve a good relationship with business associates, political people, or volunteers, until they have forgotten you are handicapped."

That is courage.

GEORGE A. "PAT" ROONEY

by

William B. Hopkins

Pat Rooney began his career with the giant Minnesota Mining and Manufacturing Company in 1956, at age thirty, as Area Representative in Omaha, Nebraska, for the company's Duplicating Products Division. His career moved fast. In 1959 he was promoted to Branch Manager in Milwaukee, Wisconsin, and three years later he was promoted to Advertising/Merchandising Manager for the Graphic Systems Group and was transferred to the 3M Headquarters in St. Paul.

A year later, on a wintry day in February, 1963, Rooney was on his way to a business meeting in downtown St. Paul when his Volkswagen Beetle plowed into the undercarriage of an oil truck crossing in front of him. His car was almost leveled at the windshield and Rooney was severely injured.

At a nearby hospital, doctors discovered that his spinal cord was irreparably damaged at the fifth cervical vertebra, leaving him with severed communications between his brain and his body below the shoulders — a quadriplegic.

Rooney remained hospitalized for eighteen months during

which time he underwent extensive physical and occupational therapy, all the while determined to resume his career at 3M. Incredible as it may seem, he cannot recall that he experienced any period of despair during his recovery, only occasional moments of discouragement. He credits the great support he received from his wife and three children and his religious faith for sustaining him during this difficult period.

After hospitalization ended, and during a short stay at home, Rooney became convinced that he was not yet ready for re-entry into the work force. Too many questions about his current physical capabilities and condition remained unanswered. He found the answers he needed during a two-week stay at the Sister Kenny Institute. Satisfied with the knowledge he received there about his own body and what its capabilities were, he set about trying to reclaim the job he had left behind.

In spite of his determination and "high falutin' ideas" about how he was going to "rampage right back into the business world," it did not happen that way. Initially Rooney lacked self-confidence, and neither he nor 3M really had any idea about what he could or could not do. It was a perplexing period for both the employee and employer, but both were determined to find a way to utilize Rooney's proven expertise in sales.

Using two specially-adapted "metal fingers," Rooney could dial a phone. He sharpened his salesmanship by calling potential 3M customers from a temporary office he set up in his home. His telephone approach was so successful — one of every four calls resulted in a business lead for the 3M sales force — that he was asked to develop a program to teach sales people how to use the telephone more effectively. Thus was born Rooney's new career in telephone marketing.

Today, Rooney is one of the top experts on telephone marketing in the country. Every other week he flies to cities throughout the country conducting two-day seminars for the 3M Business Products sales force, teaching them how to manage their territory through use of the telephone — how to set up appointments with business decision-makers.

Another project which Rooney conceived and developed is referred to as "Telephone Marketing." The program, initiated in 1976, employs seventeen people and is conducted in 3M's fifteen largest branch offices. The job of these "inside salesmen" is to contact customers individually, ask about their concerns, listen carefully, and then provide a corporate response to their needs. This service illustrates that even giant companies do care about people, thereby developing customer loyalty. Because Rooney has proven to 3M that it is a person's ability, not his disability that counts, five of these fifteen "inside salesmen" are people who have a physical disability. One of the top salespeople in this program was a Chicago woman who is a quadriplegic, disabled by polio.

Because Rooney is a self-confessed workaholic, he has little chance for participation in civic affairs. He does, however, find time to devote to matters intended to improve the quality of life for the handicapped. He has served on the Board of Directors of the Sister Kenny Institute for a number of years and is a past chairman of the Board. He was also a governor-appointed member to the Minnesota State Council for the Handicapped for several years, serving one term as chairman. He has received many awards and citations, including the Rose and Jay Phillips Award presented by Courage Center.

Rooney has a deep desire to help handicapped people achieve their life goals, but he believes his time as an individual can best be used as a loner. He feels that by doing a good job at 3M, he is most effective. The company's excellent experience in working with him to help him find his employment niche is making the company more and more willing to hire other people with physical disabilities. He feels that if he had failed in surmounting his physical problems at 3M, other people with handicaps would have had a much more difficult time in crashing the employment barriers of this giant corporation.

When he began his comeback in employment, there was much doubt about his worth, among many 3M executives. They saw the wheelchair and not the man, in spite of the fact that they were willing to give him a chance. Because Rooney has led the way, few people at 3M today put limitations on what handicapped people can do.

"I have found myself getting involved with organizations that have the capability of doing some real good for a lot of people," he said. "But I'm not a 'let's get together with all the handicapped people' type of guy.

"I really feel I can do more by working with the people they have to work with, and that's the able-bodied. I feel my greatest impact is being as 'normal' as I can be in business dealings with able-bodied groups. I think it shows them that even though I may do some things differently, I am still effective."

Rooney believes that a change in society's attitudes toward the handicapped can take place only with a change in the attitudes of the handicapped themselves. "One of the most damaging attitudes that some handicapped have is their absolute unwillingness to compromise," he said. "But if you try to force people into doing what you want them to do, your efforts will not last. Militancy does the cause no good. Aggressiveness is a fine asset but it has to be tempered with good sense and persuasion. There are many people who are easy to persuade to help you when your cause is just. But there are certain people in the world you're not going to dominate. A lot has been done in the last few years for the handicapped as compared with before. It has been the difference between day and night and that's a tribute to the handicapped themselves."

Rooney's story is one of courage. It is a story of a man who was as disabled as one can be and yet live. He had the drive and determination to bring his body back to maximum efficiency under the circumstances. Even though his physical needs require the assistance of an attendant around the clock, he has been able to train himself to shave and eat unassisted. He wants no one to do the things for him that he can do himself. He could have given up but such is not his way of life. He could have resigned himself to a life of inactivity and taken whatever society was willing to give him to subsist. He would have no part of it. He wanted desperately to go back to work at the 3M Company and become independent again. He is a man with drive and courage.

Today, Rooney is a successful businessman by any standard of measurement. He feels good about himself, his family, his job. He travels daily back and forth to his nearby office in Richfield where he conducts his business with the assistance of a secretary and a personal attendant. He is a sports "nut," once having sat through a Chicago Bears football game in −36 degree weather. He maintains a keen interest in handball and has attended several national handball tournaments.

Pat Rooney, the victim of an unfortunate accident which nearly cost him his life, was deprived of much of his physical activity. It has been said that most of what we do is twenty per cent physical and eighty per cent mental. The story of Pat Rooney can lead one to believe that this is indeed true.

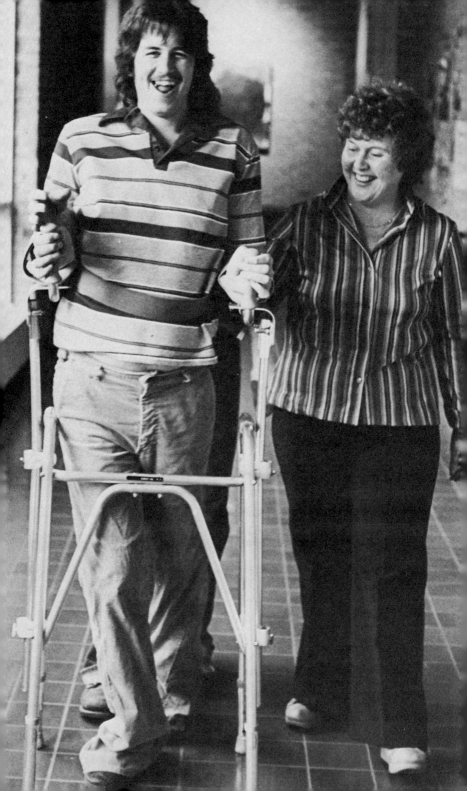

THE COURAGE STORY

by

W. B. Schoenbohm

The Courage Story is a story of daring, vision and dedication toward one goal: helping people with physical disabilities to help themselves. The thirteen individual stories in this book are stories of personal triumph over tragedy.

The personal history of Michael Dowling, for example, symbolizes the Courage Story. In 1880, Dowling, a fourteen-year-old youth, suffered the loss of both legs and one arm as the result of exposure during one of the worst blizzards in Minnesota history. Nevertheless, he fought to regain self-sufficiency and became prominent as a teacher, banker, legislator, and public speaker, inspiring thousands of other disabled individuals.

The concern of people like Dowling prompted citizens to incorporate the Association for Crippled Children in 1928, to provide education, rehabilitation and recreational services for handicapped children. In 1947 the Association was renamed the Minnesota Society for Crippled Children and Adults (MiSCCA), and its programs were broadened to include disabled adults.

Opposite: Courage resident with therapists

Meanwhile, in 1938, the Association had experimented with a ten-day camping session which would dramatically change the course of the organization's history. Jennie Bordewich Dowling, widow of Michael Dowling, working virtually without guidelines, organized a camping adventure for physically handicapped children, near Hinckley.

The camping program was expanded and moved in 1946 to another leased site near Marine-on-St. Croix. A permanent new residential facility called Camp Courage was built by the Society in 1954 on the shores of Cedar Lake, about fifty miles northwest of the Twin Cities. Courage North, a second residential camp, was opened in 1971.

In 1973, a dream came true for many physically disabled people, their families and friends, with the opening of Courage Center, a comprehensive rehabilitation facility. Located on seven and one-half acres of gently rolling hills in Golden Valley, Minnesota, not far from downtown Minneapolis, the Center is headquarters for a regional network of some seventy programs serving approximately 15,000 handicapped people annually throughout the Upper Midwest.

The Center is helping people with disabilities in their quest for greater independence, self-sufficiency and a chance to improve themselves in body, mind and spirit. Identification of the word "Courage," with the wide array of services offered, has become firmly established in the public mind. In recognition of that fact, the name of the organization was officially changed to "Courage Center" in 1978, its golden anniversary year.

Selection of the new name was almost inevitable. The Center's most widely known program, Camp Courage, serving more than 800 campers each season, was already a household term in Minnesota with a growing reputation in the entire region. Camp Courage is unique. Its uniqueness grows out of the close, warm relationship of campers and counselors, and out of its life enrichment programs which are enhanced by the beautiful natural surroundings.

Among the facilities of this 275-acre, barrier-free camp are the

Opposite above: Courage Center, Golden Valley
Opposite below: Camp Courage, Maple Lake

barnyard and native animal zoos, nature museums, self-guiding trails, fragrance garden, photography studio, radio room, library, and the ceramics and lapidary departments. Special "land pontoons" have been developed to enable campers in wheelchairs to venture into the woods to study nature. Two seventeen-acre islands are used for overnight camping: Humphrey Island, named in honor of Vice President Hubert H. Humphrey, and Winther Island, given by Dr. and Mrs. Conrad P. Winther.

The camping program began as a service to people with physical disabilities, but soon broadened to include children and adults with speech, hearing and vision disorders. In 1968, separate speech and hearing facilities were added to Camp Courage. Now, speech and hearing clinicians and support staff work intensively, helping campers with communication problems, meshing the objectives of both camping and therapy.

Camp Courage is a model of what a residential camp for people with disabilities can be. It is the camp's philosophy that the way a person feels about his or her disability is probably more important than the disability itself. With its unique facilities, programs and goals, Camp Courage provides opportunities for the lives of campers to be enriched physically, emotionally, intellectually and spiritually.

The second residential camp, Courage North, is located at Lake George, near Itasca State Park. The property was a gift from Lydia and Walter H. Deubener, St. Paul, of their ninety-five-acre former summer estate, called "Deep in the Pines." Through a program of building and remodeling, Courage North has been expanded and enlarged, making it completely accessible to campers with disabilities.

One of its special features is a leadership camp for teen-agers with profound hearing loss. Here young people who are hearing-impaired learn by doing, participating in all aspects of planning their camp program.

In addition to the two residential camps, Courage Center sponsors more than twenty day camps for children with disabilities in Minnesota and neighboring states.

130   *Opposite:* Camper at Camp Courage Barnyard Zoo

Camping is an extremely important facet of Courage Center's program, but there are dozens of others. The Center houses a comprehensive rehabilitation complex, a gymnasium-auditorium, a pool, a library, cafeteria, administrative offices, and a transitional residence for severely disabled young adults.

The Center's construction was assured and speeded by a 1968 bequest of more than a million dollars, the largest in the organization's history, from the estate of Benjamin Bunge, a farmer-investor from Eitzen, Minnesota. The gift was followed by support from other generous friends of Courage: individuals, foundations and organizations.

One type of activity that has blossomed since the 1973 opening of the Center is the Sports, Physical Education and Recreation program. Athletic activities are of vital importance in improving attitudes as well as health, and in breaking down communication barriers.

The Twin Cities Rolling Gophers wheelchair basketball team affiliated with Courage Center in 1975. One of the nation's largest wheelchair sports groups, the Gophers include nearly seventy men and women athletes competing in ten sports. The Center also sponsors other wheelchair teams: The Twin Ports Flyers (Duluth-Superior); The River City Ramblers (St. Paul); and The Chippewa Valley Wheelers (Eau Claire, Wisconsin).

Other athletic and recreational activities include conditioning classes, swimming, volleyball, softball, football, soccer, archery, track, floor hockey, wheelchair square dancing and blind square dancing. A program specifically for the recreation of youngsters with disabilities is the Saturday Club.

Adjoining Courage Center is Courage Residence, completed in 1975, a short and long-term living facility for severely disabled young adults who have good rehabilitation potential. Residents benefit from a combination of physical restoration programs, counseling, group activities, vocational, recreational and social services.

It is the aim of these programs to help residents achieve greater independence and self-sufficiency, building a bridge for them to move back into the community. Residents enter into a contract

Opposite: Rolling Gophers prepare to shoot

system defining goals for their stay. Goals may include improving their health, going to college, training for a vocation and finding a job.

Gains have been dramatic. A recent follow-up study of former residents established that prior to moving into Courage Residence they had an average hospital stay of thirty-one days per year. After responding to Courage Center's rehabilitation programs, these same residents reduced their average annual number of days in the hospital to seven.

Beneficiaries of Courage Center services range from the very young to the elderly. The Therapeutic Preschool offers special education with advanced methods of therapy for as many as seventy-two children, ages one to five. These children benefit from a daily program of physical, occupational, speech and hearing therapy. Special emphasis is given to involving parents and family in each child's program.

The immediate objective of the Therapeutic Preschool is to prepare handicapped youngsters for attendance in public schools or at a special school in the community. Its longer range goal is to reduce the handicapped child's need for institutional care or attendant care at home by increasing his or her ability to become independent.

Adults with disabilities participate in a wide variety of individual outpatient therapy services at Courage Center, as well as homebound therapy. Unique among these is rehabilitation engineering, in which the combined skills of trained technicians and volunteers help to increase the independence of rehabilitation clients and residents. Technicians and volunteers evaluate each individual and then design and produce whatever custom-made apparatus might be needed to enhance that person's self-sufficiency.

The Center's technological work evaluation program unites rehabilitation engineering with vocational evaluation and computer technology. This program prepares adults with severe physical disabilities for training and jobs in the computer industry, allowing them to make their own direct contribution to society and to gain more economic independence.

Opposite: Preschooler in therapy

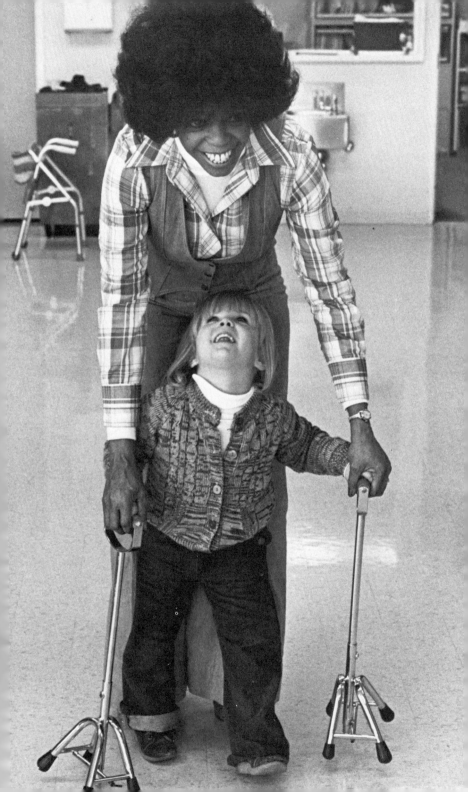

Courage Homecrafters is a vocational rehabilitation service for men and women who cannot work outside their homes because of a disability. The program helps men and women with handicaps to develop the skills they need in order to create income-producing craft items, leading them to greater financial independence. Homecrafters retail outlets include the Courage Center Gift Shop, the downtown Minneapolis Skyway Gift Shop and special sales at shopping centers and homes.

Another Courage Center program, the international HANDI-HAM System of amateur radio, is helping to broaden the world of hundreds of disabled people throughout the country. The program helps people attain their amateur radio licenses and equipment. Amateur radio is more than just talk. Through the HANDI-HAM System, a world that might be bounded by four bedroom walls can be expanded to the farthest corners of the globe. In addition to personal growth, it offers the opportunity for operators to perform vital emergency public service.

The remarkable growth and development of Courage Center programs through the years have been possible because of broad community support: financial support from individuals, foundations and organizations, including our own Courage Auxiliary; volunteer support from hundreds of dedicated volunteers throughout the region; and support from members of the professional health community, who continue to recommend Courage Center services for their clients. They, too, have shown courage and vision, and have helped to make the Courage Center dream a reality.

And the dream goes on: Courage Center's most recent five-year plan, outlining some of the unmet needs which are being considered for further development, is entitled, "The Courage to Dream."

As Courage Center steps into the future, it does so in the faith that when an institution addresses the needs of human beings with confidence and courage, the blessing of God and the continued support of a caring public will accompany its efforts. That's what the Courage Story is all about.

Opposite: HANDI-HAM operator

CONTRIBUTING WRITERS

AND

EDITORS

Janet S. Burns was born in Minnesota and has lived in Duluth since the age of seven. She is a graduate of the University of Minnesota and of Columbia University Graduate School of Journalism.

After raising three children, she returned to writing several years ago, and she deeply enjoys it. She has been a journalist with the Duluth *News-Tribune* since February 1970 and is former city editor.

Her husband was the late Herbert M. Burns, Duluth attorney. Her two sons are also attorneys, and her daughter is a public relations consultant. Burns has seven grandchildren.

Kathryn Christenson, Grant Coordinator at Gustavus Adolphus College in St. Peter, Minnesota, is a free-lance writer whose poetry and articles have appeared in periodicals and anthologies.

A Wisconsin native, she received a bachelor's degree from University of Wisconsin-Eau Claire and a master's degree in English from University of Minnesota. She edited the book, *Granlund: The Sculptor and His Work* and has taught English and women's studies classes.

With her husband, Ron, and children, Rolf and Abigail, she

lives in St. Peter, where she is active in college and community activities.

Dorothy Collins is Minnesota Editor of the Fargo-Moorhead *Forum*. A versatile journalist, she covers the Minnesota Legislature and northwestern Minnesota politics as well as writing a column on gardening.

She has received many awards, including a certificate of recognition for her contribution as a reporter covering the Moorhead School District; the R. L. Wodarz Award in Horticulture from North Dakota Horticultural Society; and an award of merit from Minnesota Horticultural Society. In 1975 she was honored by the YWCA as Centennial Woman of the Year.

A graduate of University of Washington School of Journalism, Collins was editor of the University *Daily*. She currently serves on the board of Fargo-Moorhead United Way and of Clay County Cancer Society. She has one son, Ross, a graduate student at University of Warwick, England.

Gareth Hiebert, feature writer whose "Oliver Towne" column appears in the St. Paul *Dispatch* and *Pioneer Press,* began his career with those newspapers as a campus correspondent in 1939 while attending the University of Minnesota. He started writing his column in 1954 and has also been city editor.

Interesting people, neighborhoods, buildings, restaurants and historic sites are among the topics that fill his columns and feature stories. A world traveler, he has written several books about his travels and about St. Paul.

Born in Minneapolis, Hiebert grew up in New Ulm, graduated from the University of Minnesota in 1943 and saw action during World War II in the Battle of the Bulge. He is retired as a Lieutenant Colonel, Reserve, with thirty-three years of service. He and his wife have two daughters and two sons.

William B. Hopkins, Public Affairs Director at Courage Center in Golden Valley, Minnesota, is a member of several state and national groups which promote improved access for people with physical disabilities.

Born in Oklahoma, he served in the United States Army during World War II, later graduating from Southeastern Louisiana University and doing graduate work at Louisiana State. Since moving to Minnesota, he has been chief advocate for many landmark statutes to improve the mobility of people with handicaps and was originator of the Access Minnesota program of the State Council for the Handicapped.

Hopkins has had a notable career in Kiwanis, holding offices at the local, division and Minnesota-Dakota District level. He and his wife, Joan, have two children, Jon and Mary.

Daniel Huff is a feature writer for the Tucson, Arizona, afternoon newspaper, the *Citizen*. He has been a member of its staff for three years.

He holds a law degree from University of Arizona, Tucson, and a degree in journalism from Arizona State University in Tempe, where he was named the outstanding graduate in journalism in 1970. He was recently honored by an organization of his colleagues as one of the outstanding feature writers in Arizona.

Huff counts photography as one of his hobbies. With his wife, Gina, he lives in Tucson.

Carol Lacey is a reporter for the St. Paul *Pioneer Press* and a community faculty member at Metropolitan State University, St. Paul. She does independent communication, women's studies and children's studies consulting, writing and research. Her column, "Little Folks," geared to parents and others interested in children, appears weekly in the *Pioneer Press*.

Lacey's degrees include: a B.A. from Concordia College, Moorhead, in music, English and German; an M.A. from the University of Minnesota in journalism and political science; and a Ph.D. in American Studies from the University in 1980.

She and her husband, Bob, and daughter, Kristi, live in Shoreview, where she also teaches piano students.

James Martin, editor/writer at the Metropolitan Council in St. Paul, has pursued careers in both teaching and communications. Before assuming his present position in January, 1980, he was Publications Coordinator for Courage Center. He does free-lance writing as well.

After graduating from Harvard in 1962, Martin spent two years as an English teacher with the Peace Corps in Niger, West Africa. He subsequently taught English at St. Paul Academy and Breck School in the Twin Cities and also in Washington, D.C. and Brazil. In 1970 he received a master's degree in English from the University of Minnesota. He has also been a public lecturer and World Press Institute program coordinator.

Martin lives in St. Paul with his wife and two children.

Kelvin W. Miller is head of Primarius, a Twin Cities planning and promotion firm which he founded in 1978.

A 1973 graduate of Gustavus Adolphus College in St. Peter, Minnesota, he joined the College staff as administrative assistant in the arts, band and choir tour manager and Executive Secretary for G-1000, a major fund-raising activity. He received the Gustavus Adolphus Fine Arts Award in 1978 in recognition of his service.

In 1976 Miller was consultant and coordinator during the visit to Minnesota by King Carl XVI Gustaf of Sweden. He was editor of the book, *Granlund: The Sculptor and His Work*, published in 1978. He and his wife, Diane, live in Burnsville, Minnesota.

Itzhak Perlman has been called the foremost concert violinist of his generation. He performs annually with America's major symphonies, as well as with internationally known orchestras such as the Berlin Philharmonic, Vienna Philharmonic, London Symphony, Amsterdam Concertegebouw and L'Orchestre de Paris.

As a child three years of age in Tel Aviv, Israel, he fell in love with the violin. At age four, he contracted polio. Undaunted by a resulting disability that requires his using crutches, he earnestly pursued the study of his chosen instrument, came to America in his early teens and won the prestigious Leventritt Award in 1964.

Noted since that time as a brilliant solo recitalist, Perlman also performs in chamber music ensembles and is a leading recording star. His wife, Toby, and the couple's four children accompany him on his tours of major summer music festivals in the United States and abroad.

Jane Rachner has had a double vocation as free-lance writer and teacher. Among her publication credits are feature stories, fiction, poetry, humor, book reviews, professional journal articles and advertising copy.

Rachner holds a doctorate in education from the University of Minnesota, a master's degree from Mount Holyoke College and a bachelor's degree from Rockford College. She has been both a public school teacher and a visiting professor in the fields of child development and special learning disabilities.

She enjoys writing about people because of the endless variety of experiences that their life stories provide. A favorite avocation is playing with her two grandchildren.

W. B. Schoenbohm, Executive Director of Courage Center since 1952, spearheaded the establishment of Courage Center with its Camp Courage and Courage North, as well as a multiplicity of programs and services for people with disabilities. He helped found The Crippled Children's School, Jamestown, North Dakota, and was Superintendent for ten years.

A native of Iowa, he graduated from Wartburg College in Waverly and received his master's degree from State University of Iowa. He was the first Director of the University of Iowa School for Severely Handicapped Children and Assistant Director of State Services for Crippled Children.

Schoenbohm is the author of numerous articles on rehabilitation and a book, *Planning and Operating Facilities for Crippled Children*. He has helped establish and has been consultant to rehabilitation centers both in the midwest and Brazil.

Schoenbohm is the father of five children. He and his wife, Virginia, live in Golden Valley.

Robert T. Smith, columnist for the Minneapolis *Tribune*, specializes in people and human experiences. In his twenty some years in journalism, he has covered beats ranging from the neighborhood police station all the way to President Charles de Gaulle of France.

Born in Minneapolis, Smith attended the College of St. Thomas in St. Paul and was graduated from the University of Minnesota. An ensign in the United States Navy during World War II, he spent his six final months of active duty in north China.

Smith is former City Editor of the Minneapolis *Tribune*. During the Kennedy administration he was News Editor of *Time* Magazine's Washington Bureau. For five years he was Deputy Bureau Chief for *Time* in Paris.

John E. Tilton has been a newsman for half a century. After beginning his career in Iowa and Pennsylvania, he came to Minnesota in 1954 to organize a suburban group of newspapers, now known as the *Sun* newspapers.

Currently a columnist for the *Sun* group, he was its publisher until 1970. Among other civic contributions, he was instrumental in the development of the Minnesota Zoological Garden.

Tilton lives in Hopkins, is married, and has three children.

Pauline Walle has been Family and Lifestyle Editor of the Rochester *Post-Bulletin* since 1964. Before that she was with the University of Minnesota-Duluth news service and alumni office. She also served briefly as Women's Editor of the Hibbing *Daily Tribune*.

Among her journalism awards are several first places in her section category, most recently from the Press Women of Minnesota for editing Lifestyle pages. Walle is an advisory board member for both the Rochester Community College and the Salvation Army.